This Is What You're Doing Wrong

Ian Laing

ISBN 978-0-9926717-0-9

British Library Cataloguing in Publication Data.
A catalogue record for this book is available from the British Library.

Printed by CPI Group (UK) CR0 4YY

To Mummy Laing, and to Winkle
Also, for Manny Preston.
He would have loved this.

INTRODUCTION

Everyone shut up and listen to me. My dad used to say that happiness was just blissful ignorance, and I believed him. Why would he lie? As I got older it gradually dawned on me that my dad was a miserable old tosspot and I should make a point of proving him wrong.

I have therefore decided to go through all the problems we face in society and tell you how to sort them out. Crime, education, double chins, the environment, sexism, elephant-shagging, alien invasion, you name it.

Am I educated? Am I respected? Am I super-clever? No. The best ideas are normally the simplest and intelligence can get in the way. I don't have anything particularly clever to say and no flowery way of saying it, so you'll just have to take this the way it comes.

It's easy to look at world problems as really hard and difficult, with deep-rooted hatred, loads of historical baggage and no obvious answers. Rubbish. Life is as difficult or as simple as you want to make it.

This book is one chapter long. One chapter is all you need. If you can't make your point in one chapter, stop bullshitting. Excessive evidence, chapters, and structure just waste time and bore everybody. Just tell it like it is. Remember; faint heart never fucked a pig, so let's get on with it.

I'm going to start with crime.

CHAPTER 1 AND ONLY

I robbed a bank once. It was easy. I got away with fifteen paying-in slips, three pens, a pot plant and some leaflets on buying shares. I would've liked some money but it was locked behind the counter.

The traffic in London is a nightmare so I made my getaway in a police surveillance helicopter. For the first fifteen minutes I flew around London following police cars to see how they liked it. They didn't.

To be fair, the police – British Police, best in the world, God bless'em – didn't take it lying down. As I passed Slough, the Hot-Air Balloon Unit tried to force me to land, whilst some psycho from the Hang Glider Squad tried to ram me over Windsor but the draft from my rotor blades wafted him away. As I passed junction 6 of the M4 I glanced down to see two coppers stood on the exit ramp holding a stinger across the road, bouncing on pogo sticks.

Reaching the coast I decided to stay out of sight by flying down the channel tunnel like the beardy bloke in Mission Impossible, only to find the train coming *from* France at that particular moment. It never occurred to me to get a timetable.

I hit the train so hard I was flung through the windscreen of the helicopter. The rotor blades punctured the train's fuel tank, creating a blast so massive I was propelled down the tunnel towards France. Reaching Paris in no time, I came out the tunnel like Marvello the Human Cannonball, knocking a gendarme's hat off and destroying a brand new Pret A Manger.

The fallout was severe. It took the French fire brigade three hours to cut me from the baguette rack, and the police gave me a right pasting when they got me down the station. Luckily, the train I hit was empty due to a commuter strike and so only the driver was killed.

It was during my long stay in the prison hospital that I took stock. I'd always wanted to be a master criminal. Cars, money, chicks, fame, danger, shooters, more chicks, casinos...oh go on then.

But could crime ever really ever work, or would you inevitably end up in prison or dead? Can crime ever be truly eliminated, or is it just a fact of life? Being more of a doer than a thinker I'd decided to find out for myself, but got off to a really bad start.

Luckily, the driver of the train was discovered to have been a paedophile. The French authorities had his body exhumed, chopped his balls off and hung them off the Eiffel Tower. The government then granted me early release; under the terms of their Samaritan laws I had, by killing the train driver, technically saved the life of a child. First, I had to go before le judge and swear on my mum's life I wouldn't do it again, which I did. Once out, I decided to continue my experiment.

The British Government would only let me back into the country if I agreed to wear an electronic tag. I tried telling them it would interfere with the navigation on planes and would place the lives of hundreds of people at risk. I was told the terms of my tag meant not leaving

Newbury and being home by 6pm every night, so had no business even being in an airport.

I claimed the tag was interfering with the scanning equipment in my local supermarket, costing me thirty-three quid one day for a steak & kidney pie and a pint of milk. They demanded a receipt as proof, which I couldn't provide. In the end I got some kids to remove the tag with a plunger and some Swarfega, and went underground.

There's lots of ways to make money from crime, though I didn't want to get involved in any violence. I didn't fancy the idea of becoming a professional hit-man, or protection or money lending. In the end I decided to give kidnapping a go.

Kidnapping is a bit old school now because it very often fails. Someone gets kidnapped. The family refuse to pay. The hostage is a) killed or b) released. In other words, a) life in prison or b) you look a right tit in front of all your kidnapping pals. I decided to try something different. Targeting a wealthy MP, I decided not to kidnap one of his kids, but some of his money. I then sent the following demand:

"I have £500,000 of your money. If you ever want to see it again, leave one of your children, in unmarked, non-sequential clothing by the bench next to the crazy golf course in the park. No police or the money gets it."

I also sent a picture of the money next to that morning's Daily Telegraph. Why do kidnappers always send pictures of their victims next to copies of the Sun, the Daily Mirror, or the Daily Star? What kind of message does that send? "By the way, I'm thick as fuck so feel free to try any 'funny stuff' because it'll probably work." I saw someone photographed with a copy of the Sunday Sport once. Along the top you could see the kidnapper's surname, where the newsagent had written it when sorting the papers for the paperboy.

The MP decided not to cooperate. He said he had no intention of caving in to my demands, that he did not negotiate with terrorists, and would rather have his children than the money. The public were so impressed by his strong stance and family values he got the job of Home Secretary. I, however, kept the dosh. Everybody won. Except me. And the MP.

A week later a copycat stole my money and demanded my kids in exchange. I don't have any kids, and couldn't go to the police without having to admit it was me who stole the MP's money. Shot with my own gun.

The new Home Secretary was later sacked in disgrace after being found unconscious on the lawn of his mansion with cocaine on his top lip. His trousers were round his ankles, his pants were soaked in blood and next to him was a dead hedgehog with a tangerine in its mouth.

Things had gone a bit sour but I was convinced the basic kidnapping scenario had potential. Obviously the real dream deal on the kidnapping circuit is the Stockholm syndrome, in which kidnap victims fall in love with their captors. Hollywood has used the Stockholm syndrome to dream up stories in which the captor and his captive fall in love, snog, and then join forces to rip off Daddy because he's a complete bastard anyway and all manner of humorous escapades ensue.

This was my next line of attack. Page-three models. Kidnap them, let them fall in love with me, and then, whatever, who cares? The first one I kidnapped I decided to treat nicely, allowing her to sit in the front of the van with me. After all, we were technically courting. Unable to take my eyes off her fabulous knockers I crashed the van and she escaped.

Page-three girl number two was the sexiest little thing I'd ever seen. The first time she looked at me with her big blue eyes and giggled I got a hard-on so big it knocked the van out of gear at a junction. Stalling the van, I rolled backwards into a bus. Whilst exchanging insurance details with the bus driver my new captive seized her chance. Spotting a mate of hers passing by, she wound down her window and yelled to her to record Big Brother that night as she was being abducted and would probably miss it. I poked the bus driver in the eyes to prevent a positive ID and made my getaway on foot.

I decided to give it one last go. The third went as smooth as can be. She offered very little resistance, seemed excited by my scheme, and we soon reached my hideout. We watched Friends DVDs, ate kebabs, drunk Bacardi, and painted each other's toenails. Her dad was indeed a spiteful old tosser and she was more than happy to defraud him out of some money. It was all coming true.

One night, after I'd shaved her legs, she kissed me. It was bliss. After five minutes I'd even managed to wedge my hand up her bra, but then she stopped. She "loved me to death," but I was "too chubby, too old, too hairy, and too square," for it to last. I tearfully accepted her decision, and dropped her off at Chicago Rock.

I later contacted the aforementioned MP with some anonymous advice after he became Home Secretary. As well as the anti-sleaze part of his campaign, one of his other big things was to abolish fox hunting, an animal rights commitment that later rang hollow after the hedgehog incident.

The MP, by the way, escaped prison for his antics by invoking a law from Henry the Eighth's time, permitting the clergy and members of the government to fornicate with the creatures of the King's forest.

Attempts to later rehabilitate the MP's career floundered when a videotape of the hog-hump found its way onto the internet, in which the hedgehog was first plied with cocaine, and then had his toe stamped on to get him to open his mouth wide enough to fit the tangerine in.

Hunting has obviously been banned now, with much bitterness and social upheaval in the rural community – country people calling city folk "cunts" for telling them what to do. My advice was not to abolish hunting itself, just switch the hunt onto some better targets. There are lots of brilliant targets for the hunt; people and creatures that deserve to die more than a fox. There's no childcare or social services in the countryside and there's so little for young foxes to do. The young cubs start hanging around field corners, pushing over sleeping cows, harassing rabbits, and throwing conkers at tractors. Before you know it they're raiding hen houses, sniffing sheep dip, mugging badgers, and mole-messing.

If you've never heard of mole-messing, it involves sneaking into the burrows of moles when they're out, and rearranging the furniture so when they come back they keep walking into stuff and falling over. It was only a matter of time before the ASBOs started arriving and the hunt was summoned.

Now I admit, foxes aren't blameless, and a willingness

to claim discrimination even when they're in the wrong doesn't help. A fox will kill every single chicken in the hen house when they can only eat one – behaviour bordering on ethnic cleansing.

But I maintain there are more legitimate targets. How about all these horrible foul-mouthed kids hanging around town centres and convenience stores swearing and abusing people? This is where I want to see a toff in a bright red tunic, on a horse, with a horn in his mouth.

We could televise it. Drink-drivers and joy-riders running for their lives before being caught and ripped to pieces. By the way, if somebody gets caught drink-driving, don't ban them from driving; ban them from drinking. If they cared that much about their licence they wouldn't have got pissed and got in their car. Ban them from drinking and drink-driving statistics will drop like a stone.

Rapists, unscrupulous builders who rip off pensioners, people who carry knives, burglars, drug dealers, Big Brother evacuees; the list goes on. Strip them naked, smother them in aniseed, hang a string of sausages out their bum and cram their belly button full of Pedigree Chum. Give them a five-minute head start and release the hounds.

My fascination with pond life once led me to briefly join a terrorist movement called The 5%. The idea was simple; every five years the bottom 5% of society should be culled. I know, I know; vigilante behaviour is never justified, but in some cases I think it's all right.

Our main weapon was to put small bombs in Burberry caps and blow people's heads off. The hardest part was finding the brown tartan paint to camouflage the bombs. We blew up Lidls and Bejams, and firebombed busy bus stops. The only side effect of the bus stop bombing was that we murdered loads of pensioners, for which we got a government grant.

We put arsenic in Arctic Roll, and dirty bombs in Heat magazine. We bombed a steel-smelting plant in Cumbria, which meant the prices of the huge exhaust pipes kids put on their cars went through the roof leaving them driving round with their cars making the noises they were meant to.

Unfortunately, our actions just created new problems. The building sites were now short of labour and the government increased immigration to compensate, which fuelled the far right and led to rioting. One of the lessons we learned is that every country needs a large reserve of numptys, which I'll come back to later.

How about badgers? If you don't like seeing foxes killed, how about getting the foxes and hounds to make up and start on the badgers?

Don't be fooled by Wind In The Willows. Badgers are bitter and twisted creatures who've no reason to complain, being, as they are, pro-hunting. That's right. Pro-hunting. When the hunt's on, they're out there, leaning on the fences, cheering the dogs on.

"But badgers are an endangered species!" I hear you squeal. Well it's no wonder. For a start they won't come out unless it's between three and six in the morning. It's no wonder they're starving, what the hell is open at that time? Apparently the light hurts their eyes. Well it hurts human's eyes as well. Buy a pair of sunglasses and get on with it.

When Wat Tyler led the English Peasant's Revolt to

London in 1381 it was the badgers who tipped the authorities off. Everyone who lives in the countryside knows that crop circles are the work of badgers, and the beast of Bodmin Moor is a badger in a pantomime puma outfit. During the Falklands War the local badgers acted as scouts for the Argentinian landing force.

When I was young, I thought "badger baiting" meant tying badgers to lines and using them for fishing, a mistake that got me into all sorts of trouble. For a start, they made one hell of a splash when you tossed them in, scaring all the fish away. I snapped three fishing rods trying to reel them back because they get really heavy when wet. My scheme eventually came to light when I was caught shoplifting. I was stealing ten packets of instant mash potato a day in order to tempt the badgers out of their set.

The local environmental agency went fucking berserk, as did the local badger preservation society who couldn't figure out where all the badgers had gone. They also had expensive medical feedback equipment still attached to the badgers when I threw them in. The accumulation of drowned badger corpses then began to pollute the local rivers with, amongst other things, tuberculosis, and the fish who didn't get TB choked on fur balls after trying to eat the badgers.

The things you do when you're a kid. They sent me to borstal where I got bummed twice a week but learned to speak cockney and hit people with socks filled with snooker balls. Eventually I tunnelled out, but overshot by a couple of miles and accidentally tunnelled into the local prison on my sixteenth birthday, saving the authorities the hassle of transferring me.

Notorious gamblers as well, by the way, badgers. Has anyone here ever seen badgers having a "friendly" game of cards? Exactly, unless there's money involved they're not interested. That's the main reason they don't come out during the day, they're up all night at the casino or playing poker.

Not that I've got anything against gambling. Is 24-hour gambling a good idea? I'd go further and introduce 168-hour gambling, that way you could gamble all week without a break.

Let's open up bookies in schools. This way the kids won't have to sneak out of school to have a bet. The school can take 50% of the profits, and think of the fun it would create. Markets on how long the new headmaster will last, who's going to win the tennis tournament, how many corners will be won in the second-year house football match, which teacher's got the best tits, and spread betting on the amount of chips you'll get with your dinner.

Gambling should be allowed in hospitals. That way you can spread bet on how long your relatives will last if they go in for anything serious. You can bet on which patients will be discharged first or on the length of waiting lists at the end of every quarter.

Fat people should be allowed to spread bet on the amount of weight they can lose and keep off over a twelve-month period. Most dieters lose quite a lot of weight early on, but then put it back on. If they stand to win money by keeping the weight off a lot more of them would.

My dad was a bookie for a while, but his habit of accepting each way bets on two horse races meant he didn't last long. For people like my dad and the gambling addicts, gambling is like smoking, drinking, and credit cards. It's a way of taking people's spare income off them before they hurt themselves and is kinder in the long run. I'll give you an example.

A man from Nottingham has applied for bankruptcy after spread betting on the end of the world. He had the first of September 1992, and he's been losing fifty quid a day ever since. If the world had ended he'd have picked up a cool million pounds.

Anyhoo, my third page-three kidnapping eventually made the television programme, Crimewatch.

Every week Crimewatch does reconstructions of crimes, using actors to protect the identities of the real victims. The photo-fit made me look like the fat one out of the Ant Hill Mob, and I'm sure the actor's bum was far bigger than mine, making me wonder why I even bother doing body-pump at all.

Why do they use actors to protect the real victims? What about the identities of the actors? What about their safety?

Surely the person who, for example, mugged them, saw the victim's face when they committed the crime. Why would they want to get bashful now? What they should do is get police officers to do the reconstructions to protect the identities of the actors who've been brought in to protect the identities of the victims.

Or get famous actors to do the reconstructions; everybody already knows who they are, and you might get better performances. If Arnold Schwarzenegger played the role of a jeweller from Basingstoke, robbed as he left his shop with a week's takings, the audiences would go through the roof, and the more people who watch these reconstructions the more chance of somebody remembering something.

Alan Rickman could play a London cabbie robbed at knifepoint. Tom Cruise could play a publican shot for calling last orders. If Angelina Jolie agreed to play a prostitute (missing, feared dead) you can bet your arse I'd be watching, especially if it involved some kind of soft porn simulation. The more viewers, the more crime solved.

Crimewatch is a perfect example of how powerful the media can be, whether it's television, the newspapers or movies. Is there really any evidence that movies make people more violent? Did transvestism increase after Tootsie? Did cannibalism flourish after Silence of the Lambs? Did sharks become more violent after Jaws?

The Mayor of London has decided to act. He's banned The Wizard of Oz from the capital's cinemas and video shops for sending out all the wrong messages. Going to ask the wizard for a favour breeds dependence on the status quo. The Munchkins are offensive to those who are vertically challenged, and having a "wicked old witch" implies she is wicked because she is old and therefore ageist.

Having monkeys in a film is obviously racist – allowing the BNP to claim black people are actually blue, and the witch's hat is dangerously pointy without any kind of safety warning. The witch wears no protective helmet or high-viz clothing whilst riding her broomstick, Toto never had a jab before entering Oz – creating a potential rabies breach, and the oil used on the Tin Man is four-star, not unleaded.

The disgraceful behaviour of the monkeys implies the witch, as a single mum, is incapable of bringing up her kids properly, whilst the Lollypop Guild appears to be a whites only organisation. Having a witch riding around on a broomstick, the phallic shaft of the broom handle throbbing between her legs, implies women are only happy astride a big cock and is anti-feminist. The Munchkins also appear to be universally overweight, leading to an increased risk of diabetes, cancer, and high blood pressure.

I can see where they're coming from. The Wizard of Oz traumatised me as a kid. It was the monkeys. All those monkeys orphaned with one bucket of water, yet as long as Dorothy got home nobody cared. Where was David Attenborough whilst all this was going on?

Many people failed to notice that The Wizard of Oz was actually a prequel to The Planet of the Apes. After the monkeys were turfed out onto the street a vicious civil war developed between the inhabitants of Oz and the witch loyalist monkeys, which the monkeys won and the age of the ape was born. If Charlton Heston wanted to get back, all he had to do was click his heels together and say, "There's no place like home."

Even as a kid I wasn't happy with Dorothy being able to kill the witch with a bucket of water. There was no way the witch lived that long without getting wet. Everybody gets caught in the occasional downpour, and what about hygiene? She obviously wasn't washing her hands after going to the toilet, and yet was probably responsible for cooking the monkey's tea. No wonder they were blue.

It wasn't just Dorothy who didn't want the wicked witch to try on those red slippers. Her feet must have chucked up something awful. "They're a bit tight. I better take my socks off."

"No! Rub some soap on your heel!"

The lion only went to see the wizard so he could get good at fighting. What sort of example is that for the kids?

Then they finish the film by telling you that it was all a dream. There's no such thing as a wonderful mystical wonderland where we can all escape to for a good adventure; it's all in your mind. They might as well have finished off the film with Dorothy wandering into the bathroom to find Bobby Ewing taking a shower.

Banning The Wizard of Oz is all part of the nanny state culture. The Scottish Parliament is apparently banning Deep Purple's "Smoke on the Water" because it encourages young people to smoke in the bath, whilst kids are to be banned from text messaging in case it gives them finger cancer.

If anyone did try and build a yellow brick road in this country you wouldn't be able to go and dance on it for all the speed bumps. The hospitals would be full of Munchkins with sprained ankles and concussion.

Of course, the obsession with speeding is another thing boosting crime in this country. For starters, getting people to drive 30mph is a sure-fire way to get somebody robbed or car-jacked. In America, people who come across junctions in rough areas run red lights because they'd rather get hit by a juggernaut than robbed and iced whilst waiting for a "don't walk".

The more time you spend going through an inner city, the more likely you are to get hurt. Going 60mph instead of 30mph will halve your journey time and double your safety. If you hit a speed bump at 85mph you'll take off and fly to the end of the street, leapfrogging any children in the road.

Despite this, some cities in Britain are now making some areas 20mph, with stupid little signs saying "twenty is plenty." The slower a car travels the more fuel it uses. The speed Gestapo must therefore take their share of the blame for global warming, which is going to kill a lot more people than someone driving 31mph.

In addition to this, 20mph adds massive costs to business. The Royal Mail can now only do two-thirds of the deliveries because they can only go two-thirds the speed. Each parcel sent will therefore become a third more expensive and more vans will be needed to deliver the surplus parcels and letters, increasing pollution and congestion even more and making the roads even more dangerous.

If transportation continues to get slower and slower, Phileas Fogg's claim to be able to travel around the world in eighty days will become re-outrageous; it'll take him two weeks just to drive across Portsmouth.

Driving 20mph means it takes longer to get to work and longer to get home, meaning more road rage and less time together for families. 20mph means more traffic jams and increases the temptation for married men to pick up any prostitutes they see.

Speed limits need to be increased in inner city areas to 60mph. More kids will get killed but it's the kids who are committing all the crime, so let's look at the bigger picture.

Don't slow the cars down, just make the fronts softer. Attach large extra-soft foam bull-bars so the kids have a better chance. The bull-bars should also be covered with very small ultra-clingy plungers, so the kid sticks to the car rather than bouncing off and landing twenty feet down the road.

As you can probably tell, I had rapidly lost interest in crime. Crime was for losers, and my time would be better spent fighting crime than doing it. But for my convictions for robbery, kidnapping, extortion, parole violations and sheep worrying I'd have joined the police.

My decision to turn my back on crime came down to one thing, the same thing that drove me to prove my dad wrong. I am an optimist. People nowadays spend too much time looking at the negatives and not enough time concentrating on the positives. For many people, a lattice pork pie is nice to look at, delicious, and a clever way of letting the pork breathe. To others it's a cynical attempt to save on pastry whilst charging the same price as a normal pork pie.

I had to believe that good could win, and taking the easy way out was for pricks. I decided to redeem myself by working out how to catch more villains.

Let's take burglary. Should people be prosecuted for injuring, maiming, or even killing burglars if they catch them in their home? Although many would claim the burglars were only getting what they deserved, others worry about the spread of vigilantes.

Now sitting up all night with a shotgun waiting for a burglar to come to your house is one thing, but what if he doesn't turn up? If these people were punctual and conscientious they'd have jobs and wouldn't have the need or motive to steal. You can't stay up all night, every night, and still go to work during the day; everybody needs to sleep.

The answer is pre-emptive strikes. Don't wait in your house every night for burglars that aren't coming. Go round to the house of the nearest burglar in the middle of the night, break in, and bash his brains out with a baseball bat. On the way out, help yourself to his television and any sparkly stuff you can find.

Don't use a gun though. Guns have no place in British public life, and should only be used by the army, police, armed robbers and murderers. Look at all the trouble you see in America when school kids go crazy with guns.

I had a worryingly similar experience at school. A teacher was killed and several more severely pissed off after a disgruntled student went on the rampage with a whoopee cushion. He'd been humiliated by his new girlfriend, who'd told everybody in the school he'd farted whilst she was giving him oral sex (commonly known as backdraft).

The dead woman, a lecturer in her sixties, suffered a heart attack when she took her seat in the cafeteria and sat on a cushion. Another lecturer followed through so hard her shoes came off. After being chased and cornered in the science block by dinner ladies, the lad turned the cushion on himself.

And this in a country where guns are illegal. Imagine if we ever made the mistake of America and legalised guns. In America, guns are legal for home defence, but unfortunately get used for all sorts of other stuff, mainly murdering people.

Just imagine a car full of gang members driving around LA, preparing for a drive-by, when one of them makes a terrible discovery.

"Oh no! Guys, I've brought the wrong gun! This one's only licensed for home defence!"

"Oh for heaven's sake, Tarquin! You really are a terrible arse!"

"Sorry, Humphrey, I feel like a complete nincompoop!

We'll have to go back and get the illegal gun! I don't want to murder somebody with a gun that's only licensed for home defence; I'll get into trouble!"

"Josh, turn the car round, darling."

Apart from anything else, us Brits wouldn't stand for the noise. You can get an ASBO now just for burping in a residential area, and sergeants in the army are now encouraged to mime their orders rather than all that screaming.

I got shot once, on the way home from the pub, and my dad came flying out the house to bollock the gunman for not using a silencer.

Noise pollution is such a big deal. Cars, noisy neighbours, planes flying overhead, etc. People are so noise-sensitive. I was once suspended from my local library for farting in a saucepan when even the librarian admitted it made her laugh.

But some of the worst offenders go unpunished. Flip-flops for example. How annoying is the sound of someone walking down the street in a pair of flip-flops? Not too overpowering when just one person is on the move, but what about coastal resorts? Have you ever been to Newquay when there's a surf compo on?

Thousands of people wandering around in flip-flops. The noise is deafening. The vibrations from the flip-flops probably contribute to the size of the waves they get off Newquay, thereby attracting more surfers. All of which begs the question, which came first, the surfers or the waves?

I was in Combe Martin, in Devon, last year, on my holidays, and it was pissing down. As I walked around the town my feet gradually got wetter and wetter. Not only were my feet slipping in and out of the flip-flops, the flip-flops themselves were flicking dirty water up the back of my calf muscles and splattering the bottom of my shorts. At this moment, I had two compelling thoughts. The first was, "Sod this for a game of soldiers, let's find a pub." The second thought was brilliant; a eureka moment. An idea to make me a millionaire, and give me the financial independence to live the lifestyle I yearn to become accustomed to.

Mudguards for flip-flops. The mudguards will be lightweight, plastic, and have a Velcro strap. They won't actually be attached to the flip-flop, so if it's a nice day you can just wear your flip-flops normally. When it begins to rain, simply remove the mudguard from your pocket, strap it to your leg, just above your ankle, using the Velcro slap. The mudguards will then catch the splashage. When it stops raining, remove, wipe clean, and put back into your pocket.

Other inventions in the pipeline include the Laing Anti-Kitchen System™. It includes a kitchen tray with a built in oven so you cook your dinner on your lap as well as eat it, and an armchair with a dishwasher built into the back. When it's working the chair will vibrate, giving you a relaxing massage. Next, you buy a fridge-freezer with a flat screen plasma television for a door. You then screw the kitchen cupboards to the front-room wall and buy my Laing-designed combined fish tank and washing machine. The fish live inside the door, and whizz round like fuck when the machine's on its spin cycle.

The kitchen's time is up. I have another invention concerning colds, market research, and the environment. But I'll come to that later.

How about police sirens? The amount of noise pollution

these things generate is ridiculous, not to mention the help they give criminals. If the police want to catch more villains they need to start sneaking up on them occasionally, rather than coming down the road with the siren blaring and giving the game away.

Blokes crying at football matches like pussy-whipped latte drinkers just because their team got beat, the slapping noise you can get during full-on sex, people yelling racism just to get their own way; all of these help to pollute the audio equilibrium. The vibrations from a hundred thousand whistles being blown on a march through London causes enough vibrations to affect the navigation of migrating birds and the sonar of whales, meaning the birds end up in Blackpool and the whales grounded off Canary Wharf.

Surely it would be cheaper and quieter to lay rubber pavements? Why can't we have an hour of silence every day? Wouldn't that be nice? Between 2pm and 3pm every afternoon nobody in Britain will be allowed to speak or make any kind of noise. All cars and buses must stop, no planes allowed to take off or land. All shops to shut and trains and tubes to remain static. Wouldn't that be cool? A whole hour of silence; nothing but the sound of the birds in the trees, the gushing of the rivers or a terrorist detonating a bomb.

Back to crime. A few years ago, the MSC Napoli, a massive container ship, was grounded off the Devon coast. Its cargo spilled into the sea and washed up on the beach, sparking mass looting. Beer, nappies, brand new motorbikes, you name it. What I really wanted was a batch of electric fires to fall out and electrocute all the looters. The police were apparently helpless to stop people pouring onto the beach and taking what they wanted.

You can't stop people getting on the beaches but you can sure as hell stop them getting off. Barricade all exits and wait for the tide to come in and wash the looters away. Now salvage your own arse, you thieving bastards.

I was mugged once. Mind you it took seven of them, using knives, guns, three Dobermans, a rocket launcher and a polar bear. And I had a bad back. The polar bear, by the way, was brown, because of the warmer climate we have in this country, but we'll come to that later.

The police told me that most cases of this kind were solved in the first twenty-four hours. After that time had elapsed, the chances of solving the crime were slim at best. Eager to help, I waited till the next day, and when no progress was made I went out and got mugged all over again just too keep the investigation on the boil, but to no avail.

I vowed to get mugged every day until I got justice. By the end of the month I had no money and got a good kicking when some kids who'd mugged me found my big wedge of cash was in fact a rolled up twenty stuffed with monopoly money and an i-o-u. I took to wandering rough neighbourhoods carrying televisions until I got a bite, though I had one returned when they discovered it wasn't HD ready.

I was now in too deep. With nothing left to lose in a robbery, I took to prowling the streets looking for people to mug, giving me stuff I could then use as bait. Unfortunately, my first attempted victim turned out to be an undercover copper, trying to catch the serial muggers that were making my life a misery.

We all laughed heartily down the station when I explained what I was doing. Then they charged me with theft, wasting police time, and even inventing the original mugging.

I eventually plea bargained my way out of jail by using my borstal experience and working as an undercover rent boy for three months, during which time I made loads of amazing new friends and helped expose a ring of counterfeit gays. They were all heterosexual, but pretended to be gay because rent boys were cheaper than female prostitutes.

All of which proves that sometimes the best thing to do is nothing, and some things are best left alone. The point is, I know what it feels like to be robbed, hence my earlier theory on how to deal with burglars.

All new homes should be fitted with moats and drawbridges. The moats to be stocked with bull sharks. The moats must be dug deep but only half filled, that way if a robber falls in he can't climb out, and if torrential rain causes the towns to flood the moats will take the extra water. Make sure the moats are deep, because if they overflow and the bull sharks get out a flooded house and a wet sofa will be the least of your problems.

A hungry shark goes into a plumbing store and asks if they have any seals. Boom, boom.

Of course, the police can't be too heavy-handed in fighting crime or they might accidentally kick somebody to death or shoot somebody fifty times and start a riot, and everybody knows how bad we are at dealing with those.

If people are rioting because of the police, then sending the police to handle the situation is not necessarily a good idea. We can't send the army, and using community leaders won't work. If the community listened to a word they said they wouldn't be rioting in the first place.

Only in Britain are riots so difficult to control. In South Africa, they release cheetahs and lions to chase the rioters away. In Russia they hand out bottles of vodka, mixed with floor cleaner, and within twenty-five minutes the rioters are crying and singing songs about Molly Maloneski.

In Scandinavia it's too cold to riot, and in Spain and Portugal it's too hot. In Los Angeles, riots start and continue for days before the authorities even notice the difference, and in Belgium and Austria riots only occur when everybody's cellars are overflowing with children trying to escape.

In Australia, everybody is too spread out to riot. It takes three days to get enough people together, by which point they're calmed down and gasping for a cold one. When the aborigines rioted all they had to throw were boomerangs, putting themselves at more risk than the police.

The Germans are too busy watching or making porn, the French rioters are normally on strike, and the pollution in China chokes rioters to death long before the police need intervene.

So how can we in Britain learn to handle riots better? I'll tell you. Dinner ladies.

Nobody controls a mob like a dinner lady. They're in charge, but still one of you. They understand that people need to let off steam sometimes and will even hold the spare jumpers and coats, but they know where to draw the line.

Making a rioter stand and face the wall for ten minutes is so much easier than arresting him, and plaiting their hair is the best way to calm down a rioting female. Dinner ladies can help stagger the rioters' dinner times so they can all have their tea without the riot losing momentum, and can also make sure the littler kids get their turn throwing some Molotov cocktails.

When the riot threatens to get out of control the dinner ladies can play their trump card. The whistle. You can be big enough to attack a riot van, loot a shop, or blow up a road block, but when a dinner lady blows the whistle, you know to stop what you're doing and keep very…very…still.

The dinner lady doesn't expect much. Just some fish fingers and chips, a cup of tea, crumble and custard and good gossip for half an hour and they're happy.

After riots, the mood is normally one of soul searching and the need for calm, when it should be savage recrimination. The entire borough should have electricity cut off for a week, and the worst offending tower block should be blown up by Fred Dibnah with the tenants still in it.

The reason we are so bad at controlling riots is because the police don't get enough practice. Britain is a pretty civilised kind of place and proper riots are few and far between. Training riot police is like training a footballer; there's no substitute for match practice.

This is what you do. You empty a large Category-A prison of all guards and civilians. You fill the canteen with sticks, knives, Molotov cocktails, bricks and even the odd gun, then release all the cell doors, allowing the prisoners to come out. Also leave them loads of beer and a couple of hours to get pissed up.

The riot police stand at the end of the street all facing the wall with their eyes shut, and count to thirty. After which they open their eyes, shout, "Coming! Ready or not!" and then try and retake the prison. Fatalities will inevitably occur, but riots on the streets of Britain will become a distant memory. Faced with the sight of a new ruthless British riot police, even the Spartans would drop their swords and shields and run away.

Most crime committed in this country is random and petty, but organised crime accounts for billions of pounds worldwide, and the governments seem to be fighting a losing battle. The master criminal industry is one the British have long dominated. Just watch any Hollywood blockbuster and the baddie will always talk like Dick Dastardly.

Remember when you or your mates would get caught doing something wrong by the police? Someone's dad would go down the station and go mad at the coppers. "Why don't you leave them alone! Haven't you got anything better to do? Go and catch some real villains!" I often wondered what happens when the son of a famous master criminal gets caught drinking under-age.

Fifteen-year-old Billy Blofeld gets caught drinking Skol in the park with his mates and gets arrested. Ernst Stavros comes down, cat on his arm. "Well done, officer, I admire the way you spend so much time harassing kids and leaving the real criminals alone. Keep up the good work."

The cat, by the way, was running Spectre, not Blofeld. The cat was the brains behind the operation, and employed Ernst Stavros to carry him around because he was too lazy. If Bond had just killed the cat he could have saved himself a right load of old bother.

I read a brilliant story about a redneck in Pittsburgh who

taught his cat to fire a gun in case the "Rooskies" invaded in the middle of the night. The next week he brought home some really crap food for the cat because it was on offer at the supermarket. The cat was so pissed off he shot the redneck dead. When anti-gun campaigners called once more for guns to be banned, the local rifle association argued that "guns don't kill people, cats do."

The rednecks will never give up their guns. In the States, guns are like the poor man's American Express – accepted everywhere. You don't have to be rich to blow somebody away. It's the one thing almost everybody can do, and proves that all men are created equal.

This is very dangerous and something needs to be done. It means that if guns are ever legalised in Britain it could also destroy the British class system, the backbone of our existence. The British need people to look down on, or people to despise, and the class system gives them a clearly defined framework for doing this. Without it everybody would hate everybody, without knowing why, and this lack of focus could result in anarchy.

If the average American wants to undo the damage being done by gun culture, but doesn't want to ban guns, they need to head in completely the opposite direction i.e. legalise more forms of weaponry. How about tanks? Tank dealerships should open in every town in America, giving people rich enough to buy one an edge over the people who aren't. If there's a bunch of kids outside, don't go out and reason with them, get in your tank, drive to the corner of your road and blow the little fuckers to smithereens.

Decommissioned artillery guns should also be sold to the US public, to place on their front lawn. Surely helicopter gun-ships are the best way to repel a burglar? The rich will regain the upper hand, society will remain fragmented and America safely under the yolk of the Queen.

Who is most to blame for crime, anti-social behaviour, and the breakdown of community? I'll tell you. Parents who can see no wrong in their children, and every parent in the country does it...yes you do...don't lie to me!

You all read the paper in the morning and watch the television news cursing the government for the state of the country and blaming everything on "the kids." "There's no discipline! Lock the little buggers up and throw away the key! Stick'em on a chain gang!"

And yet what happens when your kid gets caught thieving/ vandalising/ bullying/ playing truant/ fighting? "Leave him alone! He's a good kid! It's not his fault, the others made him do it! It's the other kids you need to be worried about! What about them Chapel kids? What about them Calows?" Let's go through the standard list of excuses.

One. "He got in with the bad crowd." Everybody's favourite, that one. If your child does something wrong, and there's another kid within three hundred yards, then it must be the "bad crowd" making him do it. And yet to all the other kids' mums and dads your kid is the bad crowd. All the parents are frantically blaming each other's kids for any trouble and yet if they bump into each other outside the school they all pretend to be friends and all stand around slagging the teachers off and bemoaning the mythical "bad crowd."

Enough already. The bad crowd is like the system or the boogie man, or Keyser Soze. It's a popular myth. Anyone who's seen The Usual Suspects will remember the scene in which Verbal Kint / Keyser Soze explains to Agent Kujan, "The greatest trick the devil ever played was convincing parents the bad crowd exists."

It's true. Think about it. Your kids spin you a yarn about the bad crowd. Only after you've let them off do you realise your kid was the bad crowd all along! As Verbal Kint continues, "Do you think the bad crowd comes this close to getting caught and sticks its head out? My guess is, you'll never hear from it again."

Hitler's mum went to her grave swearing Adolf was simply an impressionable art student who just wanted attention and approval. This is the company you are now in, so stop it.

Excuse number two. "My kids don't lie to me." Yes they do! That's a lie you just told right there! Fuck me, I wonder where they get it from? All kids lie to their parents. I lied to mine, I know for fact they lied to me, you lie to yours, and you can bet your arse yours lie to you. Anyone who genuinely believes their kids have never lied to them is an idiot and should have their children taken into care.

Excuse number three. "You're just picking on my kid because you don't like me." You're probably right. Maybe if you stopped going down the school and gobbing off at the teachers they might not hate you and leave your kid alone. The next time your boy is playing up, take him down the school and invite the teacher to join you in beating him to a pulp in a show of solidarity. If it's your daughter, I find nipple-cripples get the job done.

Parents stick up for their kids when they're wrong because it's much easier than facing up to what piss poor parents they are. Is it any surprise your kids take the easy way out when you do the same? Is it any wonder we produce so many criminals?

Britain has always supplied a steady stream of criminals, but very few of them are genuine master criminals. Would you like to know why? Because there's very little in Britain the British wouldn't happily see destroyed:

"Prime Minister, I have in my possession, three nuclear warheads. Unless you meet my demands, I intend to destroy Stoke-On-Trent."

"Thank fuck."

"Pardon?"

"There's a few more places you can do for me if you've got enough missiles."

"But think about the environment!"

"You think about the environment. You're the one with the bomb. Take some responsibility!"

"Okay. I'm going to hollow out Ben Nevis and use it as a volcano hideout, from which I will launch rockets and take over the world!"

"Fantastic! It'll create jobs, generate tourism, and with the billions you extort from the UN you can buy the nearest football club and build a team capable of winning the Champions League!"

"Okay, what about this! I'm going to launch my own space station, from where I will rule the galaxy!"

"Cool! Can we tack some satellite receivers onto it? My mum still can't get Channel Five in her village, it's a joke."

"Shitting hell. Prime Minister. You don't appear to be taking my threats seriously. Unless I get £1bn by tea-time I will pollute the rivers of the planet with toxic chemicals."

"Already done. Corporations do that, and pay us for the privilege."

"That's it. Fuck you lot, I'm off to America where my British accent gets respect!"

I always hoped for a Bond villain who wasn't sophisticated, but felt he should pretend to be. All his life he'd wanted to be a master criminal but could never break into the inner circle because of his background, breeding, and terrible taste in music.

Bond, having been captured, would be brought before the villain, and find him sat in front of the fire, in his shell suit and Homer Simpson slippers, listening to Michael Bolton's greatest hits, volume two.

"Mr Bond, would you care for an After Eight mint? Or maybe some of these mini Swiss rolls, they're really nice, I like to suck the butter-cream out of them first. A drink? I'm afraid I've run out of Martini, but I've started buying these boxes of wine from Morrisons. It's good stuff; six pound I paid for this box and it tastes just as nice as the pricey stuff."

The cat would shit on his chair when he wasn't looking, and his main henchman would be unavailable, as he had Thursdays off to play badminton. In the end Bond would get him locked up on a technicality; his car tax was out of date, or he'd get a pull from the TV licence detector van over the massive monitors in his volcano.

Still the debate rages about how we can fight crime. Am I getting any nearer to a conclusion? Let's hope so. Surely education is the answer. Educate the children, my god won't somebody pleeeeeeeeeeeeeeease think of the children!

No. No, no, no, no, no. Fuck education and fuck the kids. Education in the wrong hands is just as dangerous as ignorance. Like pouring water on a Gremlin or slipping the ring on your finger whilst in Mordor, education can bring out the worst in the nasty.

People in their late teens and early twenties are prone to being psychotically unstable and comically convinced of their cleverness because they passed a few A-levels. Educating these specimens is downright irresponsible. In fact, formal education for anybody under the age of twenty-one is pointless.

Any education before the age of twenty-one should be conducted entirely through television. Kids pay attention to television, they don't listen to teachers, so let's be practical. A world without schools will be safer, less polluted, and more educated.

If you let your children out, they're only going to fight, steal, set fire to homeless people, hang around on street corners mugging other kids for their mobile phones, and sniff glue. The main reason kids are bullied or robbed on the way home from school is that they have a school to walk home from.

Keep them inside, force them onto a step machine for an hour to work off their derbies (bellies) then put them in front of the tele with a cream tea. If nothing else you're keeping them safe from the paedophiles, pit-bulls, schizophrenics, joy-riders, and gang culture waiting for them on the street, and you'll have someone handy to whack if you're in a bad mood.

It's difficult sometimes to know how to do the right thing for children. I was once thrown out the neighbourhood watch scheme when I suggested putting small children out at night in lobster pots to capture paedophiles.

With wanking, smoking, shoplifting, cycling proficiency tests, TB jabs, and puberty, children simply don't have the time for education. Spend more time educating working people to be good parents and less time weighing them down with hopes and expectations.

I've met people in my life who knew this. The secondary school I went to was on a council estate. I remember the headmaster telling the other teachers it was pointless spending too much time on the girls as most of them would be pregnant before they reached fourteen.

This headmaster was one of the first teachers in the country to abandon the safe-sex message. He'd explained the situation several times, but the amount of girls turning up to school pregnant every week showed it wasn't working.

The local education authorities poked their sad do-gooding noses in and said he was to start sex education again or else. The head tried to explain that if the girls stopped getting pregnant the social services would have nothing to do. The teachers in working class areas would have nobody to teach and the police would have no little villains to frame. Mothercare, Pampers, Cow & Gate, and half the playgroups in Britain would all go bust and people on the estate would lose their jobs. This was much worse than a few unwanted ankle-biters.

The local authorities said if he didn't restart sex education he'd be sacked.

The next day, he went into assembly, held a condom in the air and said, "Put one of these on when you're shagging or you'll end up pregnant or dead. Anyone too thick to understand this is going to die sooner rather than later so get it over and done with."

I saw my headmaster as a visionary, but sadly men of his conviction have been lost. What is the point of promoting birth control and then increasing immigration to offset the labour shortages? This is nothing more than the systematic genocide of unborn British hod-carriers. On the estate I grew up on, safe sex was locking the backdoor before you went to bed.

It's quite simple. When a working class lad needs to relax, he looks for somewhere to stick his winky. Now that might be a person, a vegetable, a tree, a log, a plug socket, or somebody's pocket. A mate of mine once removed the blades from his electric pencil sharpener, replaced them with rubber blades, stuck his willy in and turned it on.

Surely the best thing for these lads to insert their lightening rod into is a working class girl, and if they have kids, great. Think about it. Whilst these lads are shagging, they're not outside fighting, robbing, dealing drugs or stealing cars. The growth in gang violence in Britain is partly down to young girls now joining gangs. A bun in the oven is a fantastic way of taking these girls out of the gang scene for nine months at a time.

Sex education has only ever worked when the teacher actually has sex with the pupil. For some lucky, lucky, lucky, little sods this does actually happen, and yet what happens when they are discovered? The pupils and their families sue the teachers. This is outrageous.

Now I can understand the dads being furious and wanting to get something out of the deal. It's the dream of every schoolboy in Britain to be seduced in the store-cupboard by their teacher, and it's only natural to be jealous if somebody else has that dream come true. If it happens to be your son, it must be doubly annoying. As a father, you're meant to educate your son about all the sexual escapades awaiting him, not getting the low-down on every kid's fantasy from your son. "Tell me, son. What was it like?"

The dad figures he'll sue the school and get some compensation. Somebody's going to pay for all the wasted hard-ons of his youth, but if anyone deserves some extra cash it's the teacher for being such a good sport.

We need to start empowering teachers to use their judgement. If they decide the best way to improve a boy's education is to ride him like a mother bitch, then let them get on with it. They are the professionals.

I had a terrible crush on my history teacher at school. I had a fantasy that whilst on my paper round in the evenings, delivering free papers, I would stumble upon her house, where she would answer the door in a Nazi uniform, with stockings and suspenders, and drag me inside for some abusive sex.

In the end, I cracked. I decided to take the initiative, hiding naked in her stock cupboard for hours until the caretaker came in and pulled me off for £1 and a custard doughnut. Ever since that day, the smell of a janitor's mop gives me an erection.

Any teacher prepared to sleep with their students should be given a medal and a new pay deal, designed to reward the dedicated pupil-shaggers (as opposed to the sad-sacks who genuinely think they're in love with a fifteen-year-old boy.) It'll get the truancy down, don't you worry about that. Sessions with prostitutes could also be offered as a prize for academic excellence. The average working class lad couldn't give a wank for his GCSEs, but he'll pass a GCSE for a wank.

Maybe the government doesn't want to get the truancy down. Maybe if all the truants and illegal immigrants started turning up for school every day the classes would be too big and screw up the class size targets. This is where unemployed hunters can once more make a contribution.

Shoot all truants on sight. Hunters should be deputised as truancy officers. You see a kid out of school, you take him down, chop his head off, and mount it on a plaque in the assembly hall. This is the kind of base psychology kids respond to.

How about state-run boarding schools? Having kids at their disposal twenty-fours a day will free up more teacher-time for spanking, wanking, and fingering. Hell, I'd even make it a subject. Boarding schools will take kids away from their thick useless parents and put them into an environment that might mould them into something other than prison food or psychiatry fodder.

Once kids reach the age of sixteen, they must get a job. All further education is to be scrapped. All further education does is produce students and God knows we don't need any more of those. Every year I pray for the computer that marks the A-level papers to break down. Nothing makes me laugh more than some Sloane booing on the tele because they can't read classics at Norwich till the following year because their marks are wrong.

If I was a computer hacker I would fix that computer every year to give A-grades to the thickest kids and E-grades to the intelligent ones. That way the thick kids will wreck the nicest universities and fail, and the intelligent will become disillusioned and drink themselves to death in the shitty college's union bar.

What we need to aim for is a happy medium. People are too opinionated nowadays and everywhere you go there is a gobby loudmouth talking rubbish. You can be fined for speeding, anti-social behaviour, and littering. Why not fine people for stupidity? I know, it's a judgement call sometimes but most of the time it's pretty clear-cut. If you fine somebody £30 every time they say or do something stupid they'll think twice before doing it again.

Only people convinced they have something intelligent to say will dare open their mouths. Rich but thick people who have nothing clever to say will not be perturbed by regular thirty pound fines, but think of it as wealth redistribution.

Crass, raucous stupidity is now a serious problem in the UK. Just because a thought pops into your head doesn't mean you have to say it. Just because a thought enters your pudding-like brain doesn't mean it's clever. Everything you've ever fucked up in your life started with a thought in your brain. Your brain then convinced you it was a good idea and then sat in your head laughing as you careered towards another life changing balls-up.

Your mind is not always on your side, and doesn't care about the consequences of the shit that falls out of your mouth. Stop, count to ten, and think it through. Be honest with yourself. Do you have a proven track record of sublime genius or mind blowing clever-cloggery when it comes to the crunch? If not, what are the chances of miraculously developing this ability now?

Don't risk it. There is a dignity in being quietly thick that you won't find in being a gobby embarrassment. Once you've said something stupid the damage is done.

Stupidity officers must patrol the pubs, cafés, restaurants, and public transport, to weed out stupid comments. Radio talk-show hosts and political television presenters should be deputised to give out fines to those polluting the airwaves with their retardally charged drivel.

For persistent offenders, the ultimate sanction. A vow of silence. Ban people from talking for a year. It's their own fault; they had their chances but refused to take them. Now they can take time to reflect on their stupidity and the damage they've done to our collective karma. If they can't keep quiet, wrap an elastic band around their vocal cords until the vow is finished.

At this point I would like to make an important distinction – stay with me. Stupidity in its right environment is a good thing. Stupidity when channelled properly can be good. Stupid people being stupid is okay, it's when they try to be clever the problems start. And what made stupid people think they were clever? Interactivity.

Years ago, it was simple. The BBC told everybody what we thought, and we were happy with that. It was the BBC for Christ's sake! People were stupid and needed to be told what to do. That's why we invented television; to tell people what to do.

When I watch the news or current affairs programmes I want to be told what is happening and then move on, but

I can't, because of the constant breaks to "read some of your e-mails."

"Dave from Basingstoke thinks all Muslims have smelly feet and that's why they take their shoes off to pray, to air them off. Another e-mail here...Rashid from Barnsley says Christians have smellier feet, and that's why they keep their shoes on, because they are too embarrassed to take them off. Okay, keep your views coming..."

"I think Pixies Wonky-Woo-Woo Plum Fairy-Face Spunk-Trifle is a wonderful name for a child; it must be so cool to have show-biz parents, says Sarah from Stockport."

"John from Bristol thinks we should tell the jocks to get stuffed if they want independence," whilst, "Doris from Bromley thinks it's nice to see Cliff Richard back in the chart for the fifth consecutive decade – I'd like to see how many of today's bands last that long." Meanwhile, "Mercedes from Lambeth thinks education is the key, educate the children, it's so important."

Just fuck off and let me listen to people who have something intelligent or original to offer. Is it really asking so much that you keep your views to yourself rather than parading your banal, sycophantic stupidity like the FA Cup on an open-top bus parade?

It's time for people to reduce their stupidity footprint. Can't you see that publishing the views of half-wits is only encouraging the idea these people could flourish in education?

All because of interactivity. My local bank now has cashpoints that talk. They say "hello," "thank you," "wait for your money," "thank you for using us," etc.

One Friday, whilst out with my mates, I tried to take some money out of the hole in the wall and it started laughing. When I visited the machine again two weeks later with my girlfriend, it told me in a very loud voice that my account was again empty due to the two hundred pounds I'd put on my card in that "titty-bar" the other night. I switched banks.

It gets worse. People ringing into radio and television shows to poison us with their backward theories after being provoked by the resident "devil's advocate" presenter or guest.

Look up "devil's advocate" in the dictionary. It says: "To be a prick; a facetious cantankerous gobshite; a spewer of provocative verbal diarrhoea, designed to provoke loss of temper or distress in another, in the misguided belief it is intelligent, funny, or useful." I couldn't have put it better myself.

Somebody saying, "I was just being devil's advocate," should be seen as an admission of guilt, just the same as "yes, I stole it," or "okay, okay, it was me, I killed her." Anyone caught on tape claiming to have played devil's advocate should get two hundred hours community service, emptying Snot-hoover™ bags at designated flu-camps (I'll come back to this later.)

Is it okay to march around Brixton yelling, "Kill all niggers!" If it turns out you're just playing "racist's advocate?" Is it all right to yell, "Death to the Jews!" if you're just playing "Nazi's advocate?" Try forming an opinion you actually believe in and then stick to that, if you can.

The ancient Greeks had a wonderful way of deterring raucous stupidity in the young. When a young Greek pupil engaged in ill-conceived verbal stupidity, he or she was summoned to the front of the class and told to poke their tongue out. The lecturer would grab the pupil by the tongue and swing them around by it, in what historians have dubbed the "toga tongue-twister."

The toga tongue-twister was excruciatingly painful, not to mention humiliating, and taught young Greeks to think carefully before opening their mouth. This had three side effects. One, the Greeks became a race of great thinkers.

Two, the Greeks became a race of great lovers, as all youngsters developed very long, tough, flexible tongues.

Three, the Greek tradition of plate smashing in restaurants. As in modern day Britain, Greek restaurants employed students to wash the dishes. Being skint, hungry and armed with super large tongues, the Greek students would eat the leftovers, lick the plate clean and put it back in the cupboard. The restaurant goers of Athens therefore started smashing their used dinner plates to make sure next time they came the restaurant would have to give them a new, clean plate.

How can we embrace good stupidity and fight the bad kind? We'll obviously need some kind of government department, and maybe an ombudsman.

We also need to re-introduce streaming into schools. Years ago, we used to chuck all the clever kids in their own class, and all the thick ones in a divvy set. Everybody knew where they stood, and got on with it. The intelligent kids got the good teachers and the thick ones got the thick teachers. This is a very important point, so I'll repeat it. Many people don't remember, but when you got put in thick class you didn't just get the thick kids, you got the thick teacher, with the leather patches on his elbows, Lenin glasses and beetle crusher shoes.

The clever ones got the good teacher, but this is no longer the case.

Just like every profession in the world, there are good teachers and bad teachers. Mr Fuckwit became a teacher because he was bugger-all use for anything else. With the emotional maturity of a twelve year old, the dress sense of Tony Benn, breath like a bison's arse, no ambition, and a conviction for attacking the Chilean embassy with a potato bomb, there was only one option left.

Now in the right circumstances, this man is worth his weight in gold. His main talent is amusing and occupying dunces. This is why he's there. It's not to educate kids that don't want to be educated and couldn't cope if they did. The thick kids enter school at the age of five and leave at sixteen to get a job they don't need an education to do. The trick is to amuse them, keep them in one place and keep them out of trouble until they're old enough to get a job. It's easier to employ Mr Fuckwit than to pay for childcare.

The problem is that without streaming, too many of the clever kids are now being educated by somebody less intelligent, less mature and less driven than they are, and begin to get bored. The fact they can score drugs more easily, have less homework to do and get free entry into the fingering tournament is of little consolation.

This is dangerous and, again, comes from this idea that working class people can be anything they want. If everybody becomes Prime Minister who's going to clean the toilets, sweep the streets, or knock the muck up for the brickies?

Nobody, because they're all too busy getting ideas above

their station and taking responsibility for things they can't even spell. Keep quiet whilst the embarrassment is still in its early stages and you're still welcome down your local; the dog needs walking and your fantasy football league transfers have to be in by midnight. There's a good lad.

You over-educate stupid people and you're just inviting a nervous breakdown. This is understandable, but too many educated intelligent people are now having nervous breakdowns by choice.

Nervous breakdowns are a myth. A nervous breakdown is when the BNP campaign bus runs out of petrol on Brixton High Street. A nervous breakdown is being eight-years-old in a lift full of Catholic priests when it gets stuck between floors, or when an Israeli tank develops a misfire as it's passing through Gaza.

The average nervous breakdown can be cured with a game of snooker, ten pints of bitter and a curry. As the great Dr Freud once said to me, "Nervous breakdowns are like a bomb scare in a munitions factory. You could have one every day if you really wanted."

And if you're not having a breakdown, you're addicted. The "get out of jail card" for our generation. "It's not my fault! I'm addicted!" Once you have an addiction the world is your oyster.

An MP gets caught prowling Clapham Common looking for gay sex with strangers. An open and shut case of a good old fashioned pervy thrill-seeker out looking for danger, excitement, and the buzz of knowing the consequences of getting caught bumming against an ice cream kiosk when there's a close vote in the Commons. In years gone by he would have been humiliated, lampooned, exiled, and then sneaked back into the government a year later...but not anymore.

Now we have to feel sorry for this poor victim. He's addicted to putting himself into situations of high risk to himself and his career, and it's not good form to ridicule people who are mentally ill. The MP concerned gets let off the hook, but is now seen as a fruitcake loony bin and never works again.

Everybody loses. The MP loses his career, the country loses an MP who might actually be very good at his job, the public lose the chance for a good laugh, and the nocturnal common cruisers lose out on some fresh meat. This is what happens when you try and be too clever.

A sixty-year-old MP gets caught using taxpayers' money to fund sex-fuelled orgies with hookers and runs to the papers to open his heart on his "sex addiction," when there's no such thing.

You offer every sixty-year-old man in England as much sex as he wants, a gaggle of twenty-year-old call-girls to have it with and an endless supply of public money to pay for it, and every single one of them will be addicted to shagging by Christmas. Any bloke who isn't a sex addict simply isn't getting enough to build up a dependence.

There's nothing complex or socio-eco-politically-psychological going on here. The average addict simply has the means to become addicted to sex, whether it's money, fame, or the looks to get far too much action. If I was better looking, rich, good in bed and had a sturdier constitution I'd be in the Priory too. A good orgasm is ten times more addictive than crack cocaine, and will get you into more trouble.

A friend of mine once claimed that a good old-fashioned kick in the knob is what these people need, but I disagree. You stick their dick in a vice and they'll be pushing fifty quid into your top pocket and referring you to their friends.

If you're not depressed or addicted, you've got a syndrome. Take "Attention Deficit Hyperactivity Disorder." Experts now believe that seven out of ten kids now have ADHD. Is it contagious? Years ago, nobody had it. Are these kids fucking each other? How is it spreading?

Maybe ADHD is carried by head lice. We need to carry out tests. Capture some head lice and enter them in a Sudoku tournament to see how long they can concentrate.

When seventy percent of kids have got ADHD the thirty percent who haven't become the real victims. These kids are the ones that need the help and attention. Think of the alienation the non-ADHD kids are going to suffer. Maybe we should be doing more to address the needs of the Attention Deficit Hyperactivity Disorder Deficiency (ADHDD) kids.

The only people with ADHD are the lazy arse doctors diagnosing these kids:

Doctor: Right! Let's put on Sky Sports News. The transfer window closes today!

Dad: Doctor!

Doctor: What?

Dad: My kid, remember? Horrible little bastard. Won't do as he's told?

Doctor: Oh, yes. The thing to do, Johnny, is not to worry. Although it is unusual for a lad your age to have piles...

Dad: Piles? What are you talking about!

Doctor: Sorry, of course, not piles, why did I say that?

Ooooh biscuits! Okay, who had the chocolate ones!

Dad: Doctor!

Doctor: What? Oh, yes. Errrrr...attention deficiency hyperactivity disorder...or something. That's what he's got. Oh, fuck it, I forgot to do my lottery. What's the time?

The next kid who came in probably had Shop-Lifting Hyper-Light-Finger Syndrome (SLHLFS), and the next one Can't Be Fucked So Fuck Off And Let Me Play Computer Games Or I'll Stab You Disorder (CBFSFOALMPCGO-ISYD).

Of course ADHD started out as ADD. They added the hyperactivity bit later to make it ADHD when they discovered that an ADD already existed. ADD is something I have direct experience of. When I was at primary school, the caretaker told me that kids on free dinners only got milk if it was administered anally. Keen to grow up big and strong, I went along with this premise in order to get my milk. The caretaker would insert the milk bottle, then hang me upside down by my ankles and shake me until the milk was all gone.

When a teacher caught us one day the caretaker was arrested but later released after he was found to be suffering from Anal Dairy Disorder (ADD). He received £25,000 from the local education authority, who accepted responsibility for not recognising and treating his illness, whereas all I received was the derision of my kindergarten contemporaries for having farts that smelt like fudge yoghurt.

There are so many things you can suffer from now. Agoraphobics are petrified of open spaces, and lock themselves in their flat (agoraphobic is an old Celtic term meaning "work-shy bastard.")

A doctor friend of mine once tried to give birth to an agoraphobic baby. The conversation went as follows:

"Come on! You can't stay in there forever."

"Just you watch me!"

"Okay, fair enough. Just do me a favour though; I need to check your umbilical cord. You couldn't just hang it out could you?"

"No way! I'm not stupid! You must think I was born...well, any minute now!"

My task for this month is to have unprotected sex with an agoraphobic and then stay in for the rest of my life. In addition to my agoraphobia, I am now addicted to porn, the internet, vindaloo, internet porn, Sky Sports News, and non-internet porn.

I'm sick to death of having to take responsibility for my actions. I want somebody else to blame as well. I met a black, gay, Muslim, alcoholic, orphan the other day and was consumed with jealousy. As he told me himself, he's in more danger from the jealous non-diagnosed than he is from racism or the fundamentalists.

Conventional medicine or doctors are not much help either. I've only ever been to the doctor once. I was having trouble breathing through my nose and told him I was worried I had a nasal cavity. He just laughed in my face and tried to tell me that everybody has. So offended was I by his lack of understanding I ended up head-butting him. I know, I know, it was wrong. I didn't quite time it right and now my nose hurts even more.

Doctors are always banging on about not letting people do this or that because it's bad for their health, and yet they smoke, they drink beer, and they sunbathe. It's a bit like coppers committing crime in their spare time, firemen setting fire to people's houses on the way home, or alcoholics working in an Old Spice bottling plant. A doctor's job is to make sick people well, not prevent people getting sick. If nobody gets sick they're out of a job.

Doctors need to be more ruthless. Give them big shotguns and the power to shoot patients they deem to be terminal. Tell them to stop giving out drugs so willy-nilly and cut to the chase.

"Got a cough? Do you smoke? Well that's that mystery solved. Next!"

"You can't breathe? That's because you're twenty-seven stone. Now stop eating and get out of my office, you fat fucking heffalump."

"Well I appreciate you've got a cold, but that'll teach you to eat shit food and not drink enough water, won't it?"

Cold is not a word that gets used very often now. Everybody has flu or nothing at all. Avian flu, bird flu, swine flu, horse flu, zoo flu, follow flu; not a word will soon be left in the English language that hasn't been a type of flu. And every single one is a threat to the entire human race. Humans now have no immune system left and the bugs keep adapting and beating every new drug. So resourceful are these viruses the government has now asked them to help in the drive to find a cure for cancer in return for us banning cold remedies.

Luckily, I have the answer to this problem. A scheme I've mentioned a couple of times thus far; a way of benefiting from colds and flu, whilst helping the environment and doing valuable market research. A win-win-win deal.

Seventeen trillion pounds or something are lost each year in Britain due to people having days off work with "flu." This is in addition to the billion trillion million pounds spent every day on cold remedies – money that invariably ends up in the hands of terrorists, who then kill all the healthy people as they go to work.

What's even worse is that some of the ill people still go to work, still go to the pub, and still go to the shops in a deliberate attempt to spread the germs to as many people as possible, because "a problem shared is a problem halved."

In addition to this, millions of people are harassed and distracted both at home and in the workplace by market research bastards ringing us up asking us if we could spare a minute, or gorgeous dolly birds running up to you in the street with a look designed to make you think you really could have sex with them if you answer their questions. I hate these bastards and so do you.

This is what you do. When you get a cold, you report straight to a detention centre where you are quarantined in a huge hospital ward with all the other germ-ridden fiends. Once in the ward you can ease the boredom by completing market research questionnaires, tasting smoothies and fruit juices (brimming with vitamin C) and choosing which ones you prefer, taking the Pepsi challenge, and market testing films and new TV programmes. All of which can be done on terminals at your bedside. Everybody gets ill so the sample should be varied, and the views of people with lots of time on their hands are bound to be more valuable than people who are in a rush or trying to get you off the phone.

Next, an environmental scheme that could potentially save planet earth.

Colds generate snot. Lots and lots of it. Your nose runs like a tap with the stuff, meaning you spend all day blowing your nose until it's too sore to touch – think of all the toilet paper wastage. The snot sits on your chest, making you sit up coughing all night when you need your sleep. You need a way of getting all that snot out painlessly and quickly.

I have invented a simple, cheaply manufactured machine that will do the job. Whilst tucked up in your bed in your quarantine ward, in between market research activities, sleep, and meals, you can simply suck the snot out of your head with the Laing patented Snot-hoover™. The machine is based on the small hoover they place in your mouth at the dentist to suck the crap out. On my version there are two tubes. One tube goes up your nose, the other down your throat.

With having all the bacteria and germs sucked out of your system your cold will clear up much quicker, meaning less time ill, less time off work, less days lost to inactivity, less money lost, and with productivity so high immigration won't be so much of a priority.

Hay fever sufferers can come in and get drained for a small fee. The old pollen pansies are like walking snot factories, and produce snot that is of especially high quality. The amount of toilet roll saved every year alone will cut global waste by 20%.

If you have hay fever, you are probably due a break. When I was a kid, parents used to put plastic bags over the heads of hay fever kids to catch all the discharge. That's how we discovered putting plastic bags over kids' heads suffocates them. A mate of mine became so fed up with his hay fever he sliced up some Tampax small enough to fit inside his nose. The nose-pax then continued to swell until it broke his nose from the inside. It was hilarious.

How will all this help the environment? I'll tell you. All this snot can be stored and put to good use. I am conducting research at the moment on how to use the snot best, though one thought is smothering the polar ice caps with it, to see if it would set and go hard like Ice Magic, reflecting the sun's rays and reversing global warming.

The snot harvested can be used to make all sorts of products, which can be sold to finance the running costs of the wards. The money made by selling the market research to think-tanks and big business will be donated to Comic Relief. Everybody wins.

Other schemes I'm hatching include flood-proofing homes by coating the walls in a snot plasma poxy-resin made from snot, flour and recycled Sellotape.

NASA has apparently found that snot-coating shuttles helps them slip out of the earth's atmosphere much easier, like a bar of soap. Some top Swiss and Austrian skiers have recently admitted gaining an advantage in downhill skiing by coating their skis in snot (a scandal that is already being labelled "Snotgate" by the alpine media) whilst in China, snot based substances have been used to lubricate pandas' willys, resulting in a huge jump in breeding rates.

Probably the most exciting research I am conducting centres on the ability of snot to absorb CO_2. If trials are successful, I am looking at putting the snot into an aerosol form. It can then be sprayed into the atmosphere from hot-air balloons. After absorbing its quota of carbon, the snot particles will mix with the vapour in the air, making extra thick sticky clouds capable of retaining more moisture, meaning they will disperse their rain cargoes more evenly across the planet, a bit like slow-release carbohydrate.

I began working on my Snot-hoover™ project whilst fourteen years old, and tested each prototype on my stepsister. Unfortunately the hoover was initially way too strong, resulting in my sister's sinuses being sucked so hard her eyes rolled over in their sockets, meaning she could see the inside of her head. I would've asked her what it looked like but she was only two at the time.

Not being much of a businessman myself, I offered to sell my hoover to a young English inventor named Dyson. He foolishly turned down my offer and was never heard of again.

I tried finding a market for my product in the alternative therapy market, but nobody was interested. I even toyed with modifying the hoover so it could be switched into reverse/blow mode and then loaded with needles, doubling up as a portable self-acupuncture machine.

I once asked a specialist if acupuncture worked. He said, "Have you ever seen a hedgehog with a bad back?"

Alternative therapies is still a grey area. I find eating Pritt Sticks extremely effective in fighting diarrhoea, and drinking glue thinner equally effective in curing severe constipation.

This is probably not what Prince Charles had in mind when he recommended alternative medicines, in addition to his other causes, such as organic farming. Should Charles get involved in these issues? Should he use his position to influence debates of this kind? The answer to this is no.

So keen is Charles to connect with the kids, I understand

when he becomes king he wishes to be known not as King Charles, but the "aristo formerly known as prince."

Organic farming is not necessarily healthy, trust me. At least with battery-farm chickens you know what they're eating and exactly where they've been. It might not be perfect, but you know where you stand.

A friend of mine had a free-range chicken that would go into town every night and get a kebab. Is that really an improvement on a battery hen's diet? Some of them wouldn't even come home of a night. God knows where they'd been.

This idea that we should trust everything to nature is not so clever either. Nature kills millions of people in earthquakes, floods, storms and the like, and not all of these were created by man. Mother Nature is not wonderful, beautiful, or kind; she is a vicious, vindictive bitch.

Dinosaurs lived in perfect harmony with Mother Nature. Sure, they hunted and killed, but only to eat. They had no cars or oil refineries, no nuclear plants, they didn't smoke, drink, or gamble. They had no politicians, no religion, and never released a single CFC into the environment. And yet Mother Nature wiped them out, never to return.

This planet was created by a huge collision and will apparently be destroyed by one. When the end comes, do you think Mother Nature will spare the hippies, the vegans and anti-road protesters? Do you honestly think she's only going to aim the meteorites and comets at the people with four-by-fours?

Mother Nature needs to be tamed and channeled, not snuggled and cuddled like Lorraine Kelly. Letting nature get too strong is like training a grizzly bear to use a machine gun – she's already dangerous enough.

There are volcanoes, we are told, that threaten to erupt so severely they'll cover entire islands with red hot ash and cause so much tectonic mayhem that entire mountains will collapse into the sea, sending tidal waves the size of Wales crashing into Wales.

Why not just fill them with concrete? All the way to the top, and then cover the top with super glue that stretches with the explosion. The explosion will then backfire and the volcano can find out what it feels like. If the tectonic plates keep rubbing together and causing earthquakes, bung up the gap between the plates with landfill. Job done.

For those of you worrying my ribbing of Prince Charles is part of a republican agenda, relax. I love the monarchy, but not in its present form. It's too wet, too silly and superficial. The liberal era has unfortunately seen the royals paying tax, caring about the environment and divorcing every time their relationships aren't totally functional.

We don't want to see this shit from our royals. When Marie Antoinette said, "let them eat cake," the dopey French cut off her head. In retrospect, this kind of hard-nosed disdain and total lack of concern for the masses was precisely what made royalty so valuable. Now our monarchy is weak and compassionate and vulnerable and the public has no role models of strength to look to.

A good hard kick in the nuts will galvanise a working man more than somebody holding his hand, and the monarchy was the institution that understood this better than anyone.

The royals should spend less time trying to be compassionate, cool or respectable, and more time concentrating on their core strengths; drinking, gorging, puking, fighting, gambling, whoring and declaring wars on France. If I was made king tomorrow the first thing I'd do is dissolve parliament, then declare war on Prussia and stop off on my way home at King's Cross to pick up some rent boys and kebabs.

Of a Saturday, I would ride down Kensington High Street on my horse, clubbing peasants over the head as I went. I'd head down to the Embankment in my gold plated carriage, luring in prostitutes with bunches of grapes before viciously murdering them and heading on to the Rumpy-Pumpy Club for supper.

The public would love it. We could then get back to calling the royals "knobs" and "ponces" and have somebody to blame for our feelings of mild relative deprivation.

Various kings and queens carried out terrible atrocities on their own populations and massacred tens of thousands when revolt was in the air. The British public took it in good spirits because sooner or later, when things went pear shaped, they got to behead the king or queen in public and get the day off work to do so. What goes around comes around, so to speak.

If the present royal bloodline doesn't have what it takes to oppress and abuse their subjects, we need to bring in some fresh blood. I propose a spin-off of Alan Sugar's television show, The Apprentice. A reality television show, in which the winner is legally adopted by the Queen, and crowned a prince or princess, or non-gender specific royal person.

Tasks will include launching and coordinating a guerrilla

terrorist attack on a field of GM crops and flying a helicopter 150 yards to buy a pint of milk from the shops.

Ethnic minorities will be introduced to each contestant one-by-one, the contestants aim to offend them as much as possible with comments about slitty-eyes and bongo-bongo land.

Hopefuls will accompany the royal princes to a rugby match and try to eat a cheeseburger in one mouthful. Contestants will be thoroughly tested on their knowledge of divorce procedures (because this is vital), and entered into polo and fencing tournaments, after which they have to wrestle a corgi.

Contestants will join an anti-republican hunt, chasing lefties through the countryside and ripping them to pieces, before having their blood wiped across their face. Afterwards they retire to the banqueting hall for an eating competition.

Every week, one person will be evicted by Prince Philip, and put in a black cab home. At the end, the winner is crowned in Westminster Abbey. Mark my words, at least twenty television execs have just come in their pants and I await a suitable offer.

Through my sources, I've been able to acquire the line-up for the next series of Celebrity Big Brother. It reads as follows:

Alf Garnett, Ice Cube, Louis Farrakhan from the Nation of Islam, The Grand Wizard of the Klu Klux Klan, Jean-Marie Le Pen, Adolf Hitler, Peter Tatchell, Julian Clary, Benjamin Netanyahu, George Galloway, Howard Stern, Slobodan Milosevic, Robert Mugabe, Salman Rushdie, and the ghost of Jade Goody.

Events and challenges include being given nothing to eat but pork for a week and suicide bomber training, followed by a sponsored Holocaust denial. Ethnic Cleansing Weekly will be placed in the toilet to read, and Jean-Marie le Pen has to polish Tatchell's shoes for him every morning. Robert Mugabe must toil all day on the BB farm under the supervision of the Grand Wizard. To finish, a 24-hour Charity Bumathon, Muslim Miss World compo (judged by Salman) and a cricket match between the whites and the "darkies".

Top level "Fuck me, I didn't know that was going to happen!" consultants have been drafted in to train television bosses to look genuinely surprised when World War Three is declared as they wheel their barrows full of cash down to the offshore investment firm.

The next civilian series will see animal rights campaigners cutting cats' throats in return for food, vegetarians invited to eat human flesh in return for alcohol, and lesbians poisoned with anthrax and forced to suck the antidote out of Peter Stringfellow's knob.

The same source has told me about a new show the makers of Big Brother are planning. It's called Domestic Violence – Live! Cameras are to be placed in the homes of violent feuding couples, along with an unlimited supply of booze. Then watch them beat and stab the shit out of each other in another "important piece of experimental television."

Of course, in Domestic Violence Live, or DVL, you won't actually watch people doing the murder, there will obviously be a twenty-second delay in transmission so Channel Five can stop it when the killing starts. Channel

Five wouldn't want to broadcast a live murder, give them some credit. No, they'll save the murdering footage for the "DVL – Uncut" Christmas DVD.

How about Big Brother Middle East Special, in which six Israelis and six Palestinians are locked in the house together. The Israelis get their own half to live in, but also get to be in charge of the Palestinian half, and even build homes in it. The Palestinians get stones to throw at the Israelis, who get Tomahawk missiles and an Apache helicopter gunship to retaliate with.

Is there something positive to be taken from all of this? Of course there is. On a standard Big Brother series, twelve contestants are locked away where they can't do any harm to the public for up to twelve weeks. While Big Brother is on all the fuck-wits are on television or watching it. It's cheaper than prison and easier to regulate than tags. If Big Brother ran twenty-four hours per day, there would be no crime, no domestic violence, no road rage, burglaries or muggings. Big Brother truly is the opiate of the masses.

We have spin-off shows – Big Brother's Little Brother, Big Brother's Big Mouth, etc, where people talk about what's happening in the show. How about a show called Big Brother's Little Brother's Brother? Cameras will be placed in people's front rooms, or "lounges." People can then tune in to watch these people watching Big Brother or Big Brother's Mother's Brother.

We'll make the show interactive. You can have a choice of nine different families, in nine different front rooms, and switch between them as you wish. Roar with laughter as the couple from Andover argue about who's going to bath the baby because Big Brother has just asked a skinhead to wash a Muslim's feet, or watch intently as that bloke from Leeds scratches his nuts and gets a "semi" watching some bird in the hot tub. Try in vain to drag yourself away from the television as a woman from Penzance looks for her remote control when you can see it's on top of the CD player.

Okay, we seem to have got off the point slightly here, so let's draw some conclusions about education. Ask yourself some questions. Do the vast majority of kids appreciate education? Do they grasp the opportunity to learn and educate themselves, free from financial pressures? Do they remember much of what they learned at school?

The answer is no to all three. So what's the point? Teach them to read and write, by all means, but as soon as they can pick up a shovel, out to work.

Most kids are now smoking by ten years old, drinking by twelve, shagging at thirteen, and changing nappies by fourteen. You tell a fourteen year old with a family to support, who's gagging for a fag, and hasn't had a pint all week that he's got to spend his days doing unpaid study then crime is the only way to pay the bills.

Lower the school leaving age to thirteen. The education system can then concentrate on kids who actually want to learn. The days of unruly kids causing havoc on the way home from school will disappear because the sods will be at work and proper students will hurry home to study. With a hard day's work under their belt the non-academic thirteen year olds will stagger home, play on the computer for a bit or watch television, have their tea and go to bed. Quiet streets and a booming economy. Any questions?

Fat kids must be removed from school and put to work, smashing rocks and demolishing stuff on disused sites. Demolition is a great form of exercise and is good for letting off steam. Or re-introduce national service. Lock all the teenagers in barracks, get them fit and teach them to fight.

I know what you're thinking. The working classes want more than all this old school nonsense. But the truth is they don't.

The average working lad has six interests: shagging, fighting, drinking, smoking, gambling and football, though not necessarily in that order. This is not a bad thing. These are, after all, the things that keep the world ticking over. Ask them to develop a seventh interest, and the answer will be "more shagging." They couldn't give a monkey's arse about current affairs or the revolution and will only fight the system if they catch it staring at their pint.

These lads know their single days are limited. Very soon their girlfriend will be firing kids out like a clay pigeon launcher and they'll be pulling seven-day shifts on site to support the litter. So just let them get on with it. Fun for these lads is like supermarket sweep; get as much as you can whilst it lasts because the bitch is going to blow the whistle any minute now.

Stop driving working people away from their core strengths and let them get back to things they're good at, like prostitution. You can't ban boxing because it would drive it underground. Prostitution is illegal even though the consequences are exactly the same.

I've decided to use this opportunity to kick off my campaign to legalise prostitution. I've even formed my own consortium to bid for the franchise. I've decided to call it Come-a-lot, and seventy percent of our profits will go to charity. I could be the Victor Kiam of prostitution. "Hi! I'm Ian Laing! I went to a brothel once, and I liked it so much I bought the company!"

Sessions with prostitutes can help with depression, bereavement, and behavioural difficulties. Kids with ADHD have benefited from sessions with prostitutes, as have writers with writer's block, chess players seeking inspiration, golfers experiencing problems with their putting, and men whose wives don't understand them.

Unionised prostitutes can work from home and even study for a vocational qualification. Prostitutes could be deputised, able to make arrests and act as information points for tourists. People will tell their kids, "When you get lost, find a prostitute, give her your name and address and she'll bring you home."

Prostitutes could act like lollipop ladies, help pensioners across the road, collect pools coupons, or get extra money for doing odd jobs – like scouts. Many people pay prostitutes just for somebody to talk to, so why not train them as counsellors? The Samaritans are always looking for good people.

I have a question, incidentally, about lollipop ladies. If a police car is hurtling down the road, its siren blaring, everybody has to get out of the way. But what if a lollipop lady is letting some little school kids across the road? Does she have to give way? Or do the police? If the police have to stop, is it possible that criminals are paying lollipop ladies backhanders to be in the road when they are committing crimes, thereby aiding their escape? If you ever see a lollipop lady in a fur coat, be suspicious.

Sponsored prostitutes can be trained in euthanasia, conflict resolution, marriage guidance, and complex pay negotiations. They can treat clients themselves, or refer them on. They can even write prescriptions.

Come on, ladies. You've put up with enough over the years. It's no point holding all the cards if you're not going to play them. Women will be the dominant sex in the work place, the prostitutes will be taking back what money men still have; it'll be perfect.

With divorce taking half of men's money away, and the prostitutes and the taxman taking what's left, men will finally be the subservient sex. Every single penny will be in the hands of the government or bitches.

To the average bloke, the contents of a woman's knickers is like Aladdin's cave, Toys R Us, the Premier League, Disneyland and Willy Wonka's Chocolate Factory all rolled into one.

Women have complex trains of thought. Men have express elevators to their pants, where their dick yells, "Do-it!" Apparently the executive responsible for Nike's "Just Do It" advertising slogan got the idea whilst in Amsterdam, as he pondered whether or not to go down on a lady-boy.

Some prostitutes will still probably want to work outside, which will help to fight speeding and fatalities on our roads. If there were prostitutes stood on every street nobody would be driving faster than three miles an hour, so we'd no longer need speed bumps.

In addition to the re-introduction of National Service, I also propose the introduction of National Service for

Prostitutes, as an alternative. If you don't feel at home in the military, this is your way out.

Think of the benefits. Teenage pregnancy comes about because teenage girls can't stop shagging and won't take precautions. Once they become a professional prostitute their brothel will ensure their contraception and in their spare time they'll be too shagged out to get pregnant anyway. If the army takes the boys and the brothels take the girls the streets will be cleared of the flotsam and jetsam that pollute our 24/7s and pizza delivery shop zones.

I recently paid a visit to a certain European city, which I can't name for legal reasons, and decided to peruse the red-light district for research purposes. As I watched a particularly top-drawer looking bird, she span from my view and another one appeared. The platform she was stood on rotated, and had several prostitutes on it. The mechanism was modelled on the rotating display cases they put cakes on in cafes, and helped to maximise the amount of women working each window.

As I stood staring at this marvellous sight, I was approached by a tramp who claimed to have invented it and then launched into a right old cock and bull story. How he'd owned and run the largest registered prostitution agency in the city and tried to change the industry's image.

He gave money to charity, sponsored local boys' football teams, and got prostitutes to visit schools and talk to girls about condoms.

He also decided to do something for the homeless. Once a month the down-and-outs came into his brothel.

They got a bath, a shave, a hot meal and a session with a prostitute. Whilst they were doing this their clothes were washed, dried, and given back to them.

This idea was to prove his undoing. The city's homeless population quadrupled in six months. The only thing that prevents most men from becoming homeless is the harm it would do to their sex life. Homeless people are not sexy. I made love to a homeless woman once; it was like shagging a Grundon bin. I didn't tell her, obviously. She might have woken up.

The point is, most blokes would quite happily be homeless. No bills, no ironing, you don't have to cook, you can sleep till you want, go to bed when you want. But sex with fit chicks goes out the window. If you did manage to find one she'd have more holes in her arm than a colander and you couldn't afford a condom.

When it became clear they could be homeless and still get laid at one of this guy's brothels, men were charging onto the streets in their thousands. The parks looked like Henman Hill at Wimbledon, but who cared? Life was sweet.

The ladies loved it. The men happily signed the house over, the cars, everything. No marzipan layer, no glass ceiling. With women in charge, the human race would finally fulfil its potential. War, hunger and hatred would all become things of the past, putting men to shame for what they'd done to the world...in theory.

What they actually did is what all women do when released from the grip of sexist male bastards; they went on a bender. Like the pigs in Animal Farm, they simply set about enjoying all the benefits the men had.

There were also severe labour shortages because all the

men had left home and taken to the street. Immigration was increased sharply to fill the gap, resulting in increased racial tensions and men not happy about foreigners, "coming over here taking the job I voluntarily gave up and shagging the woman I left so I could screw prostitutes."

The Neo-Nazi organisations suddenly found recruitment booming. The far right became a mainly homeless, street-based movement, which made them difficult to track or monitor.

Far-right tramps were poking dog poo into the cardboard boxes of ethnic tramps and telling them to get benefits and a free house from the social.

Squatting became a real problem. People would go into their garden to water the flowers and come back inside to find the house full of middle-class homeless bankers. The original homeless people then started to complain about the streets being crowded, meaning less resources to go round. There were more people sleeping on the pavement than before the New Year sales.

The working immigrants then started to complain about being hassled by the indigenous Fascist tramp population, and grew tired of the native women coming into work late, hung-over, with breath like a bison, grabbing their arses as they were doing the photo-copying. They went home.

With the economy collapsing, inflation rampant and crime going through the roof, the public turned on the government, who in turn held the brothels responsible.

The brothels were closed down. The tramps began to miss their Sky television and were pissed off with walking everywhere, so they came home, and everything went back to normal.

And the moral of the story? As the vagrant put it, "Don't waste time on the homeless, they're all cunts."

The right-wing press will proclaim the legalisation of prostitution as the beginning of the end. This sort of thing simply isn't British. We don't stand for this sort of thing. Standards, stiff upper lip etc, etc.

This is not true, and everybody knows it. The British have a fantastic tradition of deviance, debauchery, homicidal homosexuality, adultery and perversion.

Richard the Lion Heart was insatiably gay, spending only two weeks with his wife over the course of their ten-year marriage. Whether or not the boyfriend appreciated being dragged across God knows where every time a crusade loomed is another matter.

It's time to stop fighting this urge and embrace it. Naked newsreaders, nudey lesbian cop dramas, naturist trampolining, and a cucumber up the bum for passing your driving test.

The word bi-sexual, by the way, is an old pagan word, meaning "greedy." The Kray twins were both bi-sexual. If it was good enough for them, then, quite frankly, I'm saying nothing.

If you ask the average American what they fear most about alien abduction, its anal probing. You ask the average Brit what they'd most enjoy about alien abduction you get the same answer. Abducting Brits wouldn't be difficult, getting rid of them would be the hard bit. "Okay, okay, I'll go! But only if you do that thing with the probe once more. That is fucking ace."

All new houses built in Britain must have (in addition to the moats) dungeons built in, fully equipped for whipping and sado-masochism, complete with fully tiled wet room for golden shower sessions.

The main reason Englishmen had stiff upper lips is because there was nothing you could do to them that was worse than the stuff they did to relax. They all had arses like wind tunnels and hides thicker than the upholstery on a Rolls-Royce. My old football manager used to hit his players on their bell-end with his pipe as they came out the shower. It was character building.

Part of this new liberated climate will mean the release of men and women from sexless marriages. The main reason marriages fail is because of unconditional monogamy. You have to stay loyal to your partner, even if they won't have sex with you, so you cheat on them secretly, get caught and you're in the wrong. This is nonsense. It should be okay to have an affair or use prostitutes if you aren't getting any at home.

If your partner withdraws conjugal activity, you are entitled to look elsewhere for a top-up. Sex is part and parcel of every successful marriage. You can't just withdraw it one day unannounced. Sex should be included in marriage vows. If women don't like the bit about "obey" then replace it with a sex commitment. "I promise to love, honour, and fuck to a reasonable standard, though bum-fun is optional after fifty."

Monogamy without sex is like asking a tortoise to empathise with a homeless person; totally unrealistic. If you withdraw sex, but expect your partner to be faithful, what you are basically saying is, "I've decided that you will never have sex again." You have no right to make that decision.

If your wife's fire is still burning in her fifties and sixties, even seventies and eighties, then stoke it, five times a night. God gave you a willy for one reason; going wee-wee was an afterthought. God initially gave men belly-buttons to urinate with. It was only after he perfected the sperm delivery unit that he decided, with some fancy plumbing, you could wee with it as well. The belly-button remained in case it was needed later, a bit like the spare scart-cable port on your television.

My mate's mum was a dentist. When her husband went off sex, she started bringing home the gas from work. She'd slip him a couple of Viagra in his tea, wait twenty minutes, secretly release the gas into the room, wait in the garden and then re-enter the house in a gas mask, have sex with him and when he came round she'd be waiting with some ice cream. Rape? Or a modern woman re-enfranchising her clitoris? You decide.

If you can't service your missus yourself, then help must be sought. Invite the rugby club round for a drink, slip some Viagra in the communion wine, put a card in the window of the local newsagents, drag the paperboy in one morning and spit roast him. Just do what it takes. She deserves it. And the same goes for frigid women. Put out, or let him sleep with prostitutes.

Contracts and transfer fees must be negotiated when considering marriages and family ties. Marriages must be fixed term contracts, after which you are both free agents, unless you wish to negotiate another one. If not, you are free to leave on a "Bosman." For those of you who don't follow football, a Bosman is the right to leave for nothing once your contract expires.

Men need to have more say over a woman's bits and bobs, and women must get more say over a man's. It's a perfectly reasonable idea, and all part of the liberalisation of sexuality. I suggest the creation of sex markets, where men and women can trade deficiencies or surpluses, just like oil, coffee or futures.

If a man's lovemaking is less than the required minimum, he is in deficit, and his wife is in credit. She takes her credit to the market, finds a man with a similar credit, they have sex and are both quits. I call them Shagging Exchanges.

The Shagging Exchanges will help to cement Britain's place as one of the world's main financial centres, as well as providing jobs. I'd love to be a shagging broker; the money would be good and it'd be a great way of meeting frustrated nymphomaniacs.

Would we need an exchange to cater for gay people? Or would we just mix everyone in together? After all, having their own market would just reinforce the negative view that gays are to be treated differently.

I have to confess, being straight and from a rural area I've never met many gays, at least not that I'm aware of. We always thought the attendant in my local park i.e. the parkie, was gay because he used to give us body cavity searches before we went home, "Just in case the pixies are trying to sneak out of the park in your arse." I was embarrassed to drop my pants in public when I had no pubes but when you've spent all afternoon on a red-hot slide the ice cream he used to rub on your bum to "spook the pixies" really hit the spot.

Could it be the parkie had ADD? I began to worry my bottom was emitting some kind of pheromone that attracted nonces, and took to putting Old Spice down the back of my pants, which burnt my little cheeks and just made the ice cream all the more welcome.

The parkie left to pursue a career in the priesthood, and I resigned myself to simply avoiding parks and janitors' cupboards till my tailboard matured.

Openly gay people tend to congregate in the cities, whilst the rural ones, (apart from Daffyd) tend to keep it low profile. Gay people are pretty cool from what I've seen, and seem happy to work, play, live the lifestyle and have some fun without resorting to a lot of the excesses that straight people do. It's not my bag, but so what?

Do gay people get frigid as they get older? Most gay people always strike me as being very fit – they look after themselves so much better than heterosexual people – and this fitness must prolong their sexual powers. If they remained in the closet for a long time they might have started their proper sex life later than most heterosexuals, and would want to make up for lost time. In this case they would get higher thresholds on the exchanges. Some people might see this as positive discrimination, but markets generally find their right level eventually.

As I've said, not being gay and having no gay friends means I have very little knowledge of the gay community. Do gay northern comedians do father-in-law jokes? Can you really be gay and not realise it? Is it right to "out" other gays against their will? In any other walk of life, "outing" would be seen as "grassing","dobbing","ratting", or "squealing." The fact that it involves anal sex doesn't make it different, delicate or unique. A squealer is a squealer and never to be trusted again.

The benefits of Britain's new "let-it-hang-out" approach will include helping people give up smoking. One of the reasons people don't want to give up smoking is because they'll start to eat more and put on weight. Without a fag they'll have nothing to do with their hands, so they'll eat to counter the boredom.

What about masturbation? When you're at work, and everybody decides it's time for a fag break, just say, "No thanks, I've got a much better idea." But don't go to the toilet and do it, stand outside next to the smokers, polishing your rocket, coming out with generic statements like, "God that feels better, I'm under so much pressure at the moment," and, "I'm nearly down to ten a day at the moment, though not at weekends, obviously."

Ask if any of them are considering quitting smoking. I guarantee you, by the end of the week, they all will be.

By the way, smokers should get paid less than non-smokers. We all get one hour for lunch, but you get one hour plus seven times ten minutes for fag breaks. I know people who took up smoking specifically to cadge an extra hour's worth of breaks a day.

Wanking is the nearest thing the working classes have to yoga. Why waste money on things to squeeze and balls to move about in your hands when you've got the best stress relieving tool in your pants? (This applies to women as well as men.)

As usual, we'll need to make sure it doesn't go too far. In a similar scheme in Holland, the bosses were a bit too liberal in allowing their employees time to masturbate, and the economy, again, began to suffer. Eventually they had to appoint a "Masturbation Czar." Retired policemen were touring schools, talking to seven-year-olds. "Here you go, these are called cigarettes – smoke one of these and leave your winky alone."

Smokers also generate far too much litter. I hate it when you walk down a street and see all the fag butts on the floor, and since the Government made people stand outside pubs when smoking there are more on the street than ever. If you've finished a fag and there's no bin to throw the butt in you should just swallow it. But smokers won't want to do that, will they? No, that'll be bad for their health.

Of course, the worst kind of smokers are the menthol cigarette smokers. You wankers are the worst ones going. It's not just the fact that cigarettes are bad for you, you don't even like the taste, so you get mint flavoured ones.

If you're serious about fighting carbon emissions, stick some sprigs of mint into people's exhaust pipes and then get the menthol smokers to inhale the fumes. When I lived in Lambeth in the nineties I walked home every day avoiding the thousands of piles of dog poo on the pavements. Eventually, I took to placing sprigs of mint on the piles of poo, and then waiting for the menthol smokers to pass on their way home from the pub. "It actually tastes all right with a bit of mint on it." (Gag, choke.)

But smokers do have their uses. Smokers are prepared to inhale anything if it helps them relax. If we ever do get attacked with chemical weapons the smokers will be wandering around with their gas masks on inside out. Unemployed smokers should get forty quid a day to sit by motorways sucking in all the fumes.

Back to sex.

Sexy Britain is the way forward, and once more, the animal kingdom provides many lessons we can learn. If an animal wants to have sex, they just get on with it. They don't get a room or find somewhere quiet or private. In full view of fifty other animals and BBC camera crew they just crack on. Even in front of the kids. That's why animals don't need sex education in school; they see it every day.

That's why animals don't have pornography. They don't need it. Everywhere they look animals are shagging, though watching your mum and dad going for it must be a bit disturbing, especially if you're with your mates.

Humans need to go for it wherever they see fit. On buses, tubes, in the park; just let it rip. If you work in an office go outside and have sex in the courtyard. It'll give the masturbation gang some inspiration.

It was whilst pondering this subject that I asked myself a question. Now I concede the future of the human race hardly depends on the answer, and some of you might consider this crude, but it's a question that's cost me far too much sleep over the years and I need closure, so here goes. When an elephant is mounting his lady-friend elephant from behind, is it possible he might accidentally misdirect his willy up Mrs Elephant's bottom? Elephants don't strike me as the most delicate, coordinated animals, and an elephant's todger looks a difficult thing to wield with pin-point accuracy.

Bearing in mind the size of an elephant's second trunk, I would've thought this to be a colossal faux pas, and one you'd struggle to keep a secret. God alone knows the noise a female Indian elephant would make having suddenly found that in the holding bay.

On such nights, the jungle is truly a wonderful place to be. Everything that walks, crawls, climbs or flies within a twenty-mile radius collapsing with laughter at the sound of Mrs Elephant taking friendly fire. The jungle rocking with mirth at the sound of Mr Elephant trying to play down the incident with comments like, "Sorry darling, my bad! Let me get that!"

Now, I know what you're thinking. This whole section is just a bitter and twisted rant, designed to vent the years of frustration and humiliation at my sexual inadequacy. Well of course it is. If I had a sex life I wouldn't have time to think this stuff up.

For me, the school bike sheds was a place where brewer's droop parked his chopper. A kindly dinner lady once took pity and gave me a Frenchy, but forgot to take her chewing gum out first, leaving the headmaster to carry out an emergency tracheotomy in the playground when the gum blocked my little throat.

At school I was known as "the man with the pristine penis," due to my lack of sexual engagements and subsequent constant polishing. I was given the name by a spiteful science teacher, who found out about my virginity and decided to take revenge for catching me in his lab having sex with a Bunsen burner.

My early sexual encounters were awkward and disappointing. I didn't sprout proper pubic hair until I was 27, and being able to strike a match on my groin was little consolation. My practice of taking a five-yard run-up did not win many compliments, and shouting, "Where are you lot going? Come back!" at the moment of ejaculation was seen as crass.

I never remembered to carry a condom with me, and offering to "come sideways" rarely sufficed. I slept with so many prostitutes I got cash-back and the pimps invited me on their golf day.

My last girlfriend was particularly spiteful. She used to tell people I was about as much use in bed as a chocolate teapot, a comment I found slightly vague. I know Oompa Loompas who wouldn't use anything else.

The same girlfriend was later fined £200 by local magistrates for falsely outing a straight man with a full-page advert in the local newspaper, namely me. She nicknamed my willy "mini-meat," and mocked my attempts at oral sex by telling me her clit would be wearing a red carnation to help me recognise it.

Her particular favourite was to shout, "Clean-up crew, aisle two please," when I ejaculated prematurely, and told my mates I had to put polo mints over my willy to fill out a ribbed condom.

I terminated our relationship when I caught her offering to sell my sperm to Night Nurse for a million pounds, based on the speed I fell asleep post-ejaculatum. But then my saviour arrived.

Impotence was probably the best thing that ever happened to me. Not being able to get it up was a lot less embarrassing than when I could. Women were so much friendlier when they knew I was impotent, and treated me as they might a gay man-friend.

During this period my pipe was forced to ask itself some difficult questions, and reflect on the troubles and the embarrassment it had caused me; the attention seeking, the impulsive desire to delve into bandit country, the crass insensitivity, excessive dribbling and the lack of "money-shots" when it counted.

In addition, I got through fewer underpants than before and I could watch Hollyoaks without having to put a cushion over my lap. I could go out and get drunk knowing I wasn't going to wake up the next morning with some three-eyed troglodyte and a split condom.

Until I became impotent I had no idea how much my willy had been taking out of me. I was more alert, had more energy, my hair looked great, my "writer's cramp" cleared up, and my sleep quality improved through not having to get up three times a night for wee-wees.

With less blood now needed for my erections I had more blood for the rest of me. My circulation improved and mentally I was sharp as a tack. I gained a place in my local pub's Sudoku team and got as far as the final preliminary qualifying round for Countdown, losing on penalties.

I saved a small fortune. As well as needing less toilet paper, I had no need to buy Men's magazines, pornography, internet downloads or hair gel, and no reason to buy a woman a drink. For a while life was great, but nature again decided to introduce a leveller – potentially the most dangerous invention since nuclear power.

Viagra. At the moment, impotent men are ecstatic and busily making up for lost time, whilst men who aren't impotent are taking Viagra just to last longer. This is very, very bad.

I know what you're all thinking. Here he is, telling us to have loads of sex and let it hang out, but now he's saying Viagra is bad. Well it is. Just in the same way it selected the dinosaurs for extinction, nature gave men erectile dysfunction for a reason. Why are performance enhancing drugs banned in sport, but allowed into the bedroom?

You wouldn't put a man who hadn't driven for ten years in a Grand Prix car, give an alcoholic a drink, or give a kid a machine gun to play with. It's the same thing, and using drugs to alter people's natural behaviour ALWAYS has consequences.

Inevitably stronger and stronger versions of Viagra will be formulated, creating the genuine danger of women being shagged to death by blokes with years to catch up on, and scores of men roaming the country raping and pillaging and scoffing all the Chinese.

Viagra must be banned. Nature gave men impotence to maintain some kind of harmony and Viagra will balls this up. Nature gave grandads floppy erections so their grandchildren could have a rope swing without affecting their daughter's tax credits.

Talking of raping and pillaging, I am at the moment researching a book about a horde of Vikings that landed in England around 363. They pillaged but refused to rape as they had a strict moral code forbidding it. They killed the men but left the women unscathed, even educating them about male oppression.

These gutless Nordic pussies were written out of Scandinavian history, so appalled were the longboat loonies at the thought of a Viking horde in touch with its feminine side. Their descendants settled in Britain and went on to become pricks.

This tribe are thought to be the first people ever to hit on the idea of women's rights, a process that made intelligent progress until the disastrous 1980s. Just as it looked as if women would finally break free of male domination, men played their masterstroke; feminism.

That's right. Feminism was a male invention, designed to trick women into working, and you fell for it. Now you're here, and you don't like it. Given the choice between staying at home with the kids or going to work, I know which I'd rather do.

What the hell are you thinking? Work is boring, repetitive and soul destroying, and if you can get away with not doing it, do so.

Why did women choose to show they were just as intelligent as men by matching them in the workplace, when they could have demonstrated their superior intelligence by allowing men to work and keeping their cushy housewife lifestyle they miss and now yearn for.

Women now play a greater role in the workplace, whilst men now take more responsibility for home and housework duties.

I myself have never minded doing housework (with the exception of ironing) and I enjoy cooking. A man's new jobs are no hassle for him at all. The woman for her part now has to get a job with all the hassle, grief, and stress that it brings. What's the matter, ladies? Periods, pregnancy, childbirth, breastfeeding, brittle bones and being a mother not hard enough for you?

What will you think of next? "I demand the right to be a surrogate mother to a family of elephants! Giving birth to human babies doesn't hurt enough!"

"I want to breastfeed baby piranhas, their teeth are sharper!"

"I want a drug invented that prolongs the menopause!"

And what's with all this working right up until you have the baby? Are you fucking mad? If men got pregnant, the first thing they'd do is not ring their partner or family to spread the good news, it would be to sit down to write a letter to their boss.

"Dear Boss. I've got a bun in the oven, which means I am now calling the shots. The second I can stop coming to work and still get paid I'm out of here. And don't bother employing somebody for maternity leave; give them the job permanently because we both know I ain't coming back, motherfucker. Adios."

Women! Haven't you got enough on your plate? Men are so chuffed with feminism they've now moved onto stage two. House husbands. They tricked you into working and now they're going to jack their jobs in and stay at home.

Whilst all you women in the city are sweating buckets on the tube, queuing for over-priced sandwiches and raising your hand every time you need the toilet, your modern liberated hubby is at home with his feet up, scoffing Monster Munch, watching Diagnosis Murder.

Well, congratulations. You're now in charge of every shit job in the world. I bet some of you even agreed to continue doing the ironing to help him with the transition, didn't you? Jesus Christ...

I'm honestly not saying these things to gloat. I love women. If I didn't have a penis I'd have nothing in common with the entire male race, and I want to help. Spiteful, feminist, gobby, Bolshevism has done more to screw the female race than even God himself, when he decided it'd be tremendous fun to see if a woman could squeeze a small human being out through her foo-foo.

Exactly what is sexism? There are so many grey areas. I was recently expelled from the Conservative Party for suggesting women who have a baby shouldn't also expect a present at Christmas.

Okay, okay. Everyone calm the fuck down. I'm merely making the point that women are the architects of their own failure. Women need to confront this reality or they're never going to progress.

The shit that women have gone through over the years, from the suffragettes to the modern women's lib. And what have you done with your newfound freedom? Gone on the shant. Shit-faced on Sambuca and shots that taste of Cream Eggs or footballer spunk. The first place you've headed for is not the library or the nearest political party or the city. No. Straight down the boozer to get drunk, flash your beaver and glass someone.

Women are now fat, smelly-breathed alcoholics with beer bellies and arses like stink bomb factories. London Underground now groans with the weight of transporting all the extra-fat birds to the city every day, meaning the tube has now sunk lower and needs more fuel just to get out of the tunnel, inflating costs and damaging the ozone layer.

So chuffed are women with their bellies they proudly display them, wearing cut-off tops and leggings, leaving their bellies spilling out like expanding foam spewing out from a wall cavity, showing off their stretch marks like they got them in a fight with a tiger.

Every woman in England should resign their job and get pregnant. I've actually started an organisation for all pro-womanites like me – the CRSA. With its own website, campaign HQ, and darts team, The CRSA, or Campaign to Restore Sexist Attitudes, is growing rapidly.

With modern marriage now resembling little more than the legalised armed robbery of the male species, you don't need a job to gain power, wealth, or equal billing. At least half of everything is yours whether you work or not so take the easy way out.

Why study for qualifications and strive for a career when all you really need is a bun in the oven, a ring on your finger, and a people-carrier on the drive. Once you have these three things you can throw him out and empty his bank account whilst he lives in a rabbit hutch and eats dog food.

Feminism has been a disaster for women, and like many minorities or interest groups, only now do you see that screaming abuse at white, straight, English males doesn't provide the answers to all life's problems. So ladies, let's turn the situation on its head.

The Campaign to Restore Sexist Attitudes has a seven-point manifesto:

Zero-unemployment for men.

Women to be forbidden from paid employment if they have a child under the age of fourteen.

Dinner to be on the table by seven o'clock unless you have permission.

Sex to be available a minimum of three nights per week.

Men to be allowed to visit a pub twice a week.

The legalisation of prostitution.

Women to be banned from driving or even holding a driving licence.

Occasionally, our HQ is attacked by feminists going ape-shit about our campaign. However, after attending a two-hour seminar and a game of "round the clock" they begin to see the benefits, and it's not just about avoiding work.

Years ago women complained about being trapped in the kitchen, but now many would love it. Cooking is the new rock and roll. Masterchef, Ready Steady Cook, Rick Stein, Jamie Oliver, Gordon Ramsay, and the return of Delia Smith means cooking is now just about the coolest thing on the planet.

Television is jam-packed, morning, noon, and night with cooking programmes showing you how to cook things we'd never even heard of when I was a kid. When I was at primary school, Pak Choi is what all the kids screamed when we were chasing the Vietnamese boat kiddy around the playground.

Every week on Masterchef people witter on about how deeply, deeply, deeply, deeply, deeply passionate about food they are. If you go back to being a housewife you can cook every day without the hassle and pressure of working in a restaurant. Your hubby/boyfriend/partner/co- habitee/soul mate/life sharer/family facilitator/ spunk factory will be well chuffed.

If you don't fancy cooking one day, tell him to get a take-away; he won't mind, men love take-aways!

Okay, you'll have to do some housework. Wow, some cleaning and polishing and a bit of hoovering. Change the odd nappy. Big fucking deal. You can do your shopping online, satellite television means there's loads of stuff to watch and if you can't find anything put on a DVD. Maybe surf the net for a bit, invite some friends round, do an aerobics video, AND you get to spend as much quality time with your kids as you like!

This is what happens when you kick a gift horse in the mouth. The women who embraced the feminist movement never saw the rise of satellite television, the internet, online shopping, and Nintendo Wii.

Years ago you had three channels on the gogglebox, all of which shut down in the afternoon and you had none of the other stuff. Home computers hadn't been invented, the shops closed early on a Thursday, food was crap, you spent all day washing nappies that weighed a metric ton when wet and had to walk three hours to buy some electric. The highlight of your life was getting a soda stream machine.

After a while you were lonely, bored, and unfulfilled. Your husband came home late stinking of beer, ate his dinner, watched The Gentle Touch and fell asleep on the sofa, farting. Then your husband left you for his secretary and you ended up on the game, or selling roses in Hyde Park to make ends meet. Feminism was understandable, but times have changed.

My seven-point plan ensures you get sex at least three times per week, and get shot of the wally twice a week down the pub. Less unemployed men means less crime, and if you get bored in the afternoons you can do a bit of shagging for extra money (lesbo-curious women can use their afternoons to experiment.)

Don't look at your man as the breadwinner. Look at him as a slave. "Go out and earn some money, monkey-boy. And don't come back before 5pm because I'm having the girls round this afternoon."

Stopping women driving is a great idea, and before you say it, I'm not implying that women are bad drivers. Since learning to drive women have become nothing more than a glorified taxi service. In the mornings you now have to sit in rush hour with a car full of screaming kids on the school run, dropping off before having to battle through more traffic to get to work or back home.

In the evening you can't have a few glasses of wine because you have to go and pick your kids up from parties or the town centre. Your whole life revolves around driving your sodding kids everywhere or picking your twat of a husband up from the pub to save him a taxi fare. Having a car started off as a means of independence and freedom and instead became a ball and chain.

Don't you see what you've done? All you've done is transfer the chain from the cooker to the steering wheel.

With online shopping and the introduction of a school bus service women will have no need of a car. So pissed off am I with driving that I've resolved to lose my licence with a campaign of regular drink driving. Seven or eight pints and home in my car. I wouldn't drink any more than that as I might get too drunk, crash and hurt an innocent member of the public, so I stick to an eight-pint limit.

The problem is that everybody loves me. All the people in my local pub think I'm really great and brilliant and the police look up to me. Nobody tries to stop me driving, grasses me up, or thinks to pull me over. Somehow just driving into the police station and ramming a car seems like cheating; like the ugly kid who deliberately runs slowly during kiss chase. I'll get caught soon, and then I'm free.

And another thing! What about the women who didn't want power and equality? Who genuinely love to be treated badly? What's that? They don't exist? Oh really.

In my early years I was honest and open in all of my relationships, let people into my feelings and got hurt. Badly. In return for treating them with respect I was trampled all over and left, feeling used and humiliated, normally for the ex-boyfriend. The one with whom she'd split after catching him in bed with her mum and sister; the drug dealer who'd just got out of prison for stabbing a Brownie at the village fete.

She was "on the rebound." I was sweet, but they were now going back to their boyfriend. I've got rebound stats that would make Dennis Rodman weep.

By the way, calling a bloke sweet should be grounds for justifiable homicide. If a bloke can prove a bird called him sweet whilst dumping his arse he should have complete immunity in a court of law. Blokes don't enjoy being called sweet any more than women enjoy being called cunts, so don't patronise a bloke when he's down.

It was then, that I first heard the phrase, "treat'em mean and keep'em keen." The nastier you are to them the more they come back. I looked around me, and it was true. The mean, horrible, shallow bastards had the women they wanted, whilst all the nice blokes, like me, were left behind.

I managed to persuade one of my old girlfriends to give me one last chance. I went round to pick her up in my car, beeped the horn, and when she came out I ran the bitch over. From that moment, we were inseparable. For the next couple of months she wasn't in much of a position to run away.

I called her names, forced her into degrading sex, was always an hour late for everything we were doing, shagged both her sisters, and if she ever argued back I used to wait till she was asleep and wank in her hair. She loved it.

We were happy for a while, until I came in from the pub one night and ate her. I don't mean that in an oral-sex kind of way. I actually ate her. You go out on an empty stomach, have a few jars, then a few more, come out the pub too late and all the vans and curry houses are shut, you're starving, you go home...what are you going to do?

I'd gone too far. "Treat'em mean and keep'em keen" was one thing, but run them over and eat them was pushing the envelope a bit further than it was meant to go. No decent woman would give me a chance. In the end I had to go out with the roughest bird in town.

Robert Redford played the role of the Horse Whisperer. My new girlfriend was known as the "Pitbull Bollocker" because she'd once made one cry just by shouting at it. Her name was Denise. She was a hod-carrier from Swindon, and terrorised me morning, noon, and night.

Insanely jealous, Denise once punched a police horse for looking at my arse. She came in one night, drunk, with an arm-wrestling trophy she'd just won in the pub. She went into the garden, pissed in the fishpond, ate fifteen bags of crisps, then dragged me to bed and forced me into a degrading tit-wank scenario, in which she rammed lentils into the end of my willy to see if they'd come out like buckshot when I ejaculated. I've still got one in there.

I'd met my match. When I was a kid, bullies used to give you Chinese burns or kick you in the nuts, but Denise skilfully combined the two. If I was naughty, I'd get a Chinese burn on my scrotum. There are no words in the English language to describe the pain of a fifteen-stone hod-carrier with fingers like sausage rolls wringing your scrotum out like a flannel.

She used to pass wind violently whilst we were in bed and then force my head under the covers. She blew her nose on my clean underpants and then put them back in the drawer. She'd make me watch scary films and then refuse to leave the landing light on at night. Every time she went to the toilet, she left the toilet seat up, going, as she did, standing up.

But the worst thing she did, the worst thing, was this: she'd get herself a beer from the fridge, go to the cutlery draw, get the bottle opener out, open the beer and just let the bottle-top fall into the draw, before putting the bottle opener back and shutting the draw. The draw was full of bottle tops. It used to drive...me...crazy.

I decided enough was enough, but it's difficult to know what to do. Denise was not the sort of girl that was going to respond to a quiet chat; "Let's just be friends and leave it at that." You don't just drop a bird like Denise and walk away with no injuries. I was now with her for life, or would no longer have one.

I decided to try and let her down very, very, gently. I put a cocktail of valium and sleeping tablets in her Special Brew, took her down the slaughterhouse, electrocuted her, cut her throat and hung her upside down for 12 hours. Cutting her open, I found an Illinois car number plate, a fish skeleton, and a bicycle pump. I chopped her up, made her into sausages, and threw a barbecue for the officers investigating her disappearance.

Getting back to the question (of how to get and retain the kind of woman you want) is to have two things; money and power. If you are rich and powerful you can do what you want, and everybody knows it.

Look at all these movie producers in Hollywood. Twenty-one stone with faces like photos from moon shuttles. These guys get to go out with some of the most beautiful women in America. On the night of a big movie premiere, the women are doing their hair and putting on their make-up, the movie producer gets some panel beaters in to knock the kinks out of his face.

If you're not rich or powerful the message is simple; don't pretend to be something you're not. Just be yourself. Some women genuinely like to be treated properly and don't confuse kindness with weakness. Find one of those and leave the other ones to the blokes who can handle them or are too scared to leave them, who enjoy being nagged and abused and arguing twenty-four hours a day because they then don't feel guilty about starting an affair or not coming home from the pub.

It's survival of the nastiest, and will only get worse. Spiteful people are drawn together like a magnet and a pin. They make each other's lives a misery and have fat smelly red-faced kids to paper over the cracks. These kids end up with the worst bits of both their parents, meet and marry somebody similar and then produce an even nastier kid, and on it goes.

Like fighting dogs and pitbulls, in which the strongest, most vicious dogs are mated to produce an ever more vicious breed, the human race is now becoming ever more violent and nasty, leaving the gene pool simmering and lashing out like four Klingons playing table tennis.

I propose a cull, based mainly on people under twenty-one, because they are the ones who deserve it most. Everybody without a key to the door should be executed for the following crimes:

Shop lifting.

Not pulling their jeans up over their arse.

Car theft.

Pretending to be northern when they're not, and trying to talk like a black person when they're white.

Carrying a knife.

Putting a gigantic exhaust and blacked-out windows on a Vauxhall Corsa or Citroen Saxo.

Burglary.

Shooting birds with an air-rifle.

Going on an anti-war protest.

Saying "innit" at the end of a sentence.

Graffiti.

Watching Big Brother on three consecutive days.

Being white and getting dreadlocks.

Sending more than 700 texts in one calendar month.

Having more than twenty spots on their face at any given time.

Welching on a bet.

Lethal injections will be administered at local McDonald's car parks, thereby dishing out the punishment at the venues in which they caused the most grief.

This is Darwinism at work. Survival of the fittest, death to the nastiest. If the nice people are outnumbered they need to compensate by killing the nasty. There is, however, one major problem; evolution is complete phooey and everybody knows it.

Animals are thick, stinky, and stupid, and no more evolved to suit their surroundings than humans. If humans didn't hunt, eat or experiment with animals there'd be no point even having them.

Why are animals not invisible to farmers? Why hasn't

evolution evolved sheep, cows and chickens that are poisonous to humans? Why can't sheep ride quad bikes? If I were a sheep, intent on avoiding the dinner table and the farmer jumped off his quad-bike to open the gate I know what I'd do. I'd be off down that lane like Steve McQueen.

You'd have to train the sheepdogs to ride motorbikes, with another dog in a sidecar to jump onto the quad-bike with the sheep on – "Get me in closer!"

Don't trust sheep, by the way. This idea that sheep just follow each other and don't have the intelligence to show any initiative has never fooled me. You can't follow if nobody's leading; somebody has to go first.

In years to come, when we understand more about farmyard creatures, sheep will be found at the heart of the nation's agricultural crime. You'd go a long way to find a more secretive tight-knit breed than sheep.

The main problem with evolution is that it takes so bloody long. If it becomes obvious you need legs to survive then you need them now, God-damn-it, not in a thousand years' time.

What happens if you spend a millennium evolving and don't like the results? Maybe you didn't want claws or feet; maybe you liked it in the sea.

What happens when evolution has a spurt and a generation comes out looking weird? Are they treated as fantastic specimens? Miracles of evolution? Or are they viewed as lepers, maybe even freaks? When kids are small most of them just want to fit in. Imagine being the only kid in a school of fish with legs. Try claiming you're special when your mum and dad are buying you flippers so you can keep up with other fish.

Was the evolution of humans from apes a positive thing?

Were we better off when we lived in trees? A simple existence in harmony with nature. If we'd stayed as monkeys we wouldn't have chopped down the forests; we'd have needed them to live in. The Brazilian rainforest would be the biggest housing estate in the world. We could address the need for cheap affordable housing and help the environment in one go by planting more trees. Would you rather live in a tree house or a block of flats?

If evolution had made us quicker and faster than lions and tigers and leopards, with bigger claws, we'd never have needed to invent machines, pollution, guns, tanks, nuclear stuff and cannons.

Evolution plays sick jokes on some. Homing pigeons are notoriously homesick; it's nature's way of making sure pigeons dropped off in a pleasant seaside town feel the need to fly back to a damp dingy loft in Sheffield when they'd rather be eating fish and chips by the sea.

Rather than help humans adapt, evolution has made us pathetic. A newborn human can't walk or feed itself for a year. We can't even outrun a hippopotamus, let alone a big cat, and in the sea we are known as the "monkeys on the surface" for our pathetic attempts at swimming. Humans are the only things in the sea that can make a shark laugh.

With global warming and the melting of the ice caps it stands to reason that many land based creatures, previously based in the sea, will now find their habitat completely covered in water and will have to start sprouting fins and gills in order to survive; to de-evolve. The creatures that can't de-evolve quickly enough will drown in a crushingly ironic death.

Many creatures have been preparing for this day for some time. How else can you explain hippos swimming? A creature with a belly that big and obvious dislike of exercise is not going swimming unless he's seriously worried about something, and I'm not talking about cholesterol levels.

The animals and creatures in the sea who've looked on jealously as their former species-mates ran around on dry land now get to crow for a while. But there are some creatures that really should've left the sea years ago.

Let's take seals. If I knew I was the great white shark's favourite food you wouldn't catch me within twenty miles of the coast, I can promise you that. I'd be sprouting legs by teatime. I'd go and get a job in an aquarium. Anything. I'd drive a cab if I had to. You could be coming out of a nightclub at two o'clock in the morning to find a seal in the driver's seat of your taxi:

"Shouldn't you be in the sea?"

"Fuck off! There's sharks in there! Do I look stupid...don't answer that."

If you were a seal, and you knew that sharks loved seals because they were the ultimate fat rich food, to let yourself go the way they do is suicide. When a seal sees another seal he hasn't seen for a while, does he go, "Fuck me, Neil, you've put on some weight!" Sharks are nature's way of punishing seals for the disgraceful state they get into and the outrageous amount of fish they consume. Ever since we started saving the seals the amount of fish left for us has plummeted.

Stop hitting the hard-working fisherman of Cornwall for trying to make a living; it's the seals you want to be sorting out. Don't kill them necessarily, just ween them on to kebabs or give them a good kicking when they binge, and if Attenborough gets in the way he can have some as well.

Seals don't worry too much about their appearance because all seals generally look the same. At the risk of being sealist, once you've seen one seal, you've seen them all. (When I say sealist, I mean seal racism, not third-rate celebrities.) In a world where all humans are fat we'd be less vain as well.

Corporations make billions exploiting our vanity. I got some anti-ageing cream on my birthday last year. That wasn't all I got obviously, or punches would have been thrown. But anyway, I'm putting this cream on every morning and every night. Twelve months later, my birthday comes round and lo and behold I'm one year older. What a rip-off.

And the millions of pounds spent every year on shampoo. Premiership footballers wanting to just feel good about the way they look. If David Ginola really wanted to feel good about the way he looked he should have got himself a haircut and tried winding into some fifty-fifty tackles. That would've looked real good to me.

Of course there is one member of the animal kingdom who doesn't always have a choice how it looks: the chameleon.

Chameleons don't have much use for cosmetics. They don't get to wear make-up or dye their hair; it'll just give them away. Young chameleons are notoriously nomadic because they get fed up of being the same colour every day. As they get older they're just happy to be in a routine.

If I ever had a chameleon, I would take him to a large

DIY store and show him the paint section. He'd freak. I'd buy some tins of the most exotic colours; new colours never before seen or heard of. I'd take them home, paint a section of my wall, super glue my chameleon to the floor in front of it and watch as he strained and cursed trying to blend in. "Right then. Grenada sunset. I'll give you a Grenada sunset, you bastard. Try this."

What colour is chameleon poo? Does it come out the same colour as the background so as to not give them away? If not, is it possible that chameleons have died by rolling a bum cigar as a predator passed?

Being a chameleon is hard. Young rebellious chameleons loudly proclaim their intention to go to Hollywood and become film stars, only to return home, demoralised, as they continually get lost in shot.

Every time somebody in the animal kingdom gets into trouble and doesn't have an alibi, they blame a chameleon. A grassy knoll coloured chameleon was initially blamed for the Kennedy assassination, though the racist Dallas PD later claimed it was "a negro in a costume."

A friend of mine was taken to court for running over a chameleon in his car. The skid-marks on the road showed he was doing thirty-two miles an hour in a thirty mph speed zone. The fact that he couldn't see the chameleon was no excuse for speeding. After losing his licence, my friend also lost his job and his wife left him. He vowed to kill every first-born chameleon under the age of two, but he can't find any.

During World War Two, the boffins at army HQ trained chameleons to act as government spies, or to sneak up on the Japanese in Burma and attach landmines to their vehicles. Notoriously left wing, the chameleons instead became double agents for the Russians.

They supplied numerous secrets to the dastardly Communists and revealed the identities of various British agents, as well as supplying bogus information to their British handlers. Buoyed by their success, the chameleons launched an attempt to steal the Enigma decoding machine from Bletchley Park, but a whistleblower chameleon gave the game away and the authorities were waiting for them.

Winston Churchill was beside himself. He demanded the chameleons be rounded up and shot. Fortunately for the chameleons, a kindly Oskar Schindler type figure arranged for them to be smuggled to Cuba instead, where they lived out their days in Communist exile.

Is it possible that more creatures can be trained to make a contribution to society? The US navy apparently train dolphins to plant mines on ships, whilst dogs obviously help all sorts of people, from the blind to the police.

In rural areas hedgehogs could be glued to the road and used as stingers. Sheep could be used as flood defences, being so absorbent. When Britain is flooding, release beavers into the wild and leave them loads of discarded furniture with which to build dams.

How about rats? You can eat rats. Apparently they're pretty tasty. There are millions of rats around the world. Some experts put the number at five for every human. New York now has an estimated nine million.

How about rat jerky? Somebody in New York needs to start a company, selling rat jerky in sealed foil packets to the UN, who can then send them onto the third world along with dead humans from the Cannibalism Against

Hunger Campaign. (I know, I haven't discussed this yet but I'm getting there.)

Homing pigeons should be trained as Sat-Nav programmers. When my local radio station wanted an eye in the sky slot but couldn't afford a helicopter, they released homing pigeons from designated spots with web-cams Sellotaped to their chest.

Animals also have a part to play in the new sexually liberated Britain. Having it off with farm animals should no longer be a big deal. Agricultural brothels could save the British farming industry and help people in rural areas relax and express themselves. I've always wanted to make love to a pig ever since my mate Gerald told me their tails go straight up like an aerial when they have an orgasm.

Don't just stop at animals either; necrophilia is also a good idea. Having sex with dead people is a perfectly acceptable way of unwinding after a hard day. Let's face it, most of us have tried it.

In Britain we are lucky in that we have the perfect climate for necrophilia. In hot countries the corpses go off too quickly and in cold countries the bodies freeze or are so cold you struggle to maintain an erection long enough to finish. This is why necrophilia is still rare in Scandinavia or the tropics, but flourishes in countries with milder climates like Austria and Belgium.

In Britain, global warming has made the summers cooler and wetter and the winters warmer, meaning we have just the right temperature and humidity for dead-dogging.

I'm taking a great risk telling you all this. Necrophilia is not something most people in this country are comfortable confronting, but I'd urge you to grasp the nettle. The public's lack of understanding means militant necrophilia is now rearing its ugly head, and I'd like to take this opportunity to condemn the recent wave of attacks on crematoriums by hard line necrophiliacs from the YCFDA (You Can't Fuck Dust Alliance.)

The last girl to have sex with me was arrested and charged with necrophilia; charges that were only dropped when the detective held a mirror in front of my mouth.

Does having sex with a vampire count as necrophilia? It's a difficult call to make, with that whole dead but un-dead thing they've got going on. If the answer to the question is yes, then two vampires having sex is the only time both parties can be prosecuted for necrophilia. Quite an achievement.

People could carry necrophilia cards, giving permission for their body to be used for sex after their death. The morgues could charge for providing the service, and donate a share of the profits towards making poverty history.

My step-brother also works in the death trade. He's an undertaker, in Cheltenham. Keen to liven up the whole death scene, he's gained a reputation for innovation in an industry that normally frowns upon change.

Coffins are referred to as wooden sleeping bags, and his hearse was customised by the television programme, Pimp My Ride. When the coffin is removed, the base of the car flips over to reveal a pinball machine for the lads to play on whilst the congregation are paying their respects. There's also a Play Station in the front for the kids, and a Nintendo Wii Undertaker game where you have to bury so many bodies a day to progress to the next level.

Customers are also issued with loyalty cards. When

somebody dies you get two thousand points, which can be used at supermarkets to get discounts on black ties, flowers, and CDs with music for the service.

My step-bruv's ideas got him a place on a Government think-tank where he pitched an idea to cut down on the cost of death certificates. On their thirteenth birthday, every kid was to have a barcode tattooed on their arse. When they died they could be scanned out, helping with the tracking of population migration, and eliminating the need for ID cards.

The PC members of the group called him a Nazi, and too many of the trial group used their time in the tattoo joint to also get their genitalia pierced, to the horror of their parents. My brother went back to Cheltenham.

Stupid people feel such ideas are crass and that people should be allowed more dignity in death. In reality there is no dignity in death and never has been.

I've left very clear instructions for when I pop my clogs. I want my head to be removed, pickled, and kicked off Tower Bridge by Jonny Wilkinson. I want my toe nails to be used as plectrums by Jimmy Page on Led Zeppelin's next tour. My heart is to be cooked and scoffed live on television by Hugh Fearnley-Whittingstall, and my bottom donated to Clearasil for research purposes. My left testicle is to be used as a pea in a giant whistle for ogres. I don't have a right testicle, the reason for which I'll discuss later.

I once had a dream about being killed by an ogre. Having killed me, the ogre carried my body into the garden, to the outside tap. Putting the tap in my mouth, he turned the tap on and filled my body with water. He then carried me around the garden. As he tilted me forward, the water came out of my penis. He was using me as a watering can.

For some people, dreams can be really important. They get really uptight about what they mean and any lessons they can learn. I have two dreams that just won't go away. The first involves me fishing by a lake. I catch a fish; it's a big one and things are looking up. As I begin to reel the fish in however, the corner of the fish's mouth starts to rotate. It has a fishing reel mechanism attached to the side of its mouth. The fish starts to reel me in. The dream ends with me entering the fish's mouth, calling him a "saucy bastard" and shouting that, "People won't stand for it!"

The second dream is very similar. I'm walking down a suburban street. I see a big juicy pie, the gravy is bubbling through the seams, and by the smell you can tell its steak and ale; it smells delicious. I pick the pie up and take a huge bite.

Before I can even chew, the tip of a huge hook bursts out of my cheek. There is a huge hook in the pie, which is now sticking out the side of my mouth, and I'm being hoisted towards the heavens on a fishing line. As I pass through the crowds I reach a floating ship, like a fishing boat but floating in the sky. On it sit two aliens wearing fishing hats, drinking cans of beer and holding fishing rods, one of which reeling me in for the catch. Next to them, on the deck, is a barbecue with humans gently smoking (and I don't mean having a cigarette.)

The advice I've sought seems to point to two things. The first is the pent up guilt I feel from the years spent working for my fisherman foster father, which I'll detail later. The second is my fear of the hunter becoming the hunted. This deep fear I have of humans no longer being the dominant species on this planet. Of course, we have no natural predators on this planet, and everybody knows real monsters don't exist, so often our fear is now transferred onto space, hence the aliens. Are aliens out there, and will they play nice when they get here?

I've been fascinated by space ever since I was a kid, when my grandad told me about an American baseball player called Clutch Cable, who hit a home run so high it went into space. I dreamt of travelling to the stars and finding that ball.

My grandad had some great stories. He was a corporal in the British Army during World War One. He'd been put in charge of a firing squad, shooting Germans. After a while, they had shot so many Germans they ran out of bullets. Undeterred, he began bringing the Germans out ten at a time, and blasting them with a tank.

Grandad got a commendation for initiative, but was fined a week's wages to pay for the prison yard wall to be rebuilt. Grandad also used to tell us he was captured by the Germans during the war, but survived the firing squad by lining up behind the wall instead of in front of it.

Looking back, I've an inkling grandad was a lying old sod, but the story I really wanted to believe was the one about space. We spend billions on going into space and nearly as much making programmes and films about it. Is there intelligent life out there? If there is, we're in real trouble.

Years ago we were told that the earth was flat, and to be honest, I still think it is. The whole idea of people in Australia wandering around upside down without the blood going to their head has never been properly explained by gravity.

They show us pictures of planet earth taken from space, proving the planet is round, but for all we know the earth could be flat, and its actually space that's round. Or maybe space is flat.

"Okay ensign, set a course, warp 6, engaaaaaaaaaaaaaa! What's happening?"

"We appear to have fallen off the edge of space, Captain."

"Fucksticks! Deploy parachutes!"

"We don't have parachutes sir, we're a space ship."

"Shit! That's just great! Number One, suck me off one last time."

I have visions of the Starship Enterprise careering into a huge black blanket that's been hung to signal the end of the universe. Behind the blanket are God, Satan, Allah, Martin Luther King, Frank Sinatra, and Tommy Cooper having a game of Texas Hold'em.

Of course, we need to find new planets to colonise sooner or later, because the planet's going to be hit by an asteroid, the second ice age is coming and we're all going to die.

No we're not. It's not going to happen, and I'll tell you why. For years now, we've mined all the minerals, coal, oil, and diamonds this planet has to offer. Just about everything that used to be underground is now overground. The entire weight of the planet is on the surface, creating a planet with all the structural integrity of a Ferrero Rocher. And yet people are worried what will happen if an asteroid hits the planet?

It'll be like firing a bullet at a wasps' nest. No second ice age, no freezing darkness or choking dust. Just a small popping sound as the asteroid passes straight through our hollow planet and continues on its way.

The asteroid will only hit planet earth if it manages to miss all the thousands of spare satellites and other various bits of junk floating around in space. The giant scrap metal ring around the planet is now so thick it acts like a crash barrier around the edge of a racetrack.

Is it possible that these defunct machines are still generating heat, helping to contribute to global warming? Could it be that all this junk metal is bouncing heat back towards earth or, even worse, deflecting any spare heat from the sun towards us?

Don't worry, salvation is on its way. When the aliens arrive they're bound to have the technology to solve all our problems, providing of course they're not here to eat us. If aliens did arrive they'd probably be really boring or just as stupid, petty or unremarkable as us.

Humans: So then aliens. Tonight we have a reception with Kofi Annan, David Beckham, and Barack Obama.

Aliens: Actually, we thought we'd just stay in tonight with a DVD…get a Chinese. Oh no, you go…don't worry about us. We'll be off to bed soon. It's amazing how tiring travelling can be!

Humans: This ship. The technology is breathtaking. How does it work?

Aliens: Don't ask me, I'm useless. I just turn the key and it goes. I mean, I'm not a mechanic or anything!

As a kid I remember watching movies and shows on how aliens were meant to be coming to earth and occupying humans' bodies. You had no idea they were here until it was too late. I always wanted there to be a squeamish one.

"Right, get in there."

"No way! I'm not occupying that one. He's fat and he stinks. Urr! I'm not getting in there!"

"Just get in!"

"No! He's got hay fever!"

"Tough."

"Why can't I get into a super-model or something? How about Kate Moss?"

"There's barely enough room inside Kate Moss for Kate Moss, let alone you!"

What if an alien got stuck inside someone's body? What if they couldn't get out? Maybe this is what anal probes are for, to remove aliens trapped in a human body. They suck them out like a hoover, which probably accounts for the slightly bizarre look on people's faces when they get back to earth.

What if the aliens arrived and claimed asylum? Headlines in the British press, screaming how aliens are now flocking to this planet demanding healthcare and free housing. What if the aliens were racist?

Now, as a meat eater, you have to see the irony in a race of aliens coming to earth to harvest humans for food. Our only hope would be dissident alien vegetarians breaking into human battery farms and releasing humans back into the wild.

There are bound to be a few lightweights. "I am an alien vegetarian, but I do eat fish and lorry drivers." These aliens will be seen as wishy-washy, and mocked by the Christian aliens quoting the alien bible about aliens "living off the fat of the universe."

Humans will be packaged and sold as food, including the

free-range variety. The labels will have pictures of fit healthy humans, with product descriptions: "This human was kept in a large open plan barn with Sky television and access to a state of the art gymnasium. He got five portions of fwesh fwoot and veggy-ter-bulls per day and never smoked."

Do you honestly think that aliens are going to give a monkey's about transporting humans to the slaughter-house in cramped, inhumane conditions? Any Londoner who regularly travels on the tube will be hard pushed to tell the difference. Just as humans clip the wings of chickens to stop them flying away the aliens would clip our big toes off to make balancing difficult when running.

Finally, Alien Masterchef. Domestic, everyday aliens trying to get their break in the catering trade, cooking pan fried Glaswegian with shallots and a Scouse pate.

"I find Glaswegians so perfect for this dish. The freerange Glaswegians in particular have generally consumed so much alcohol by the time they are twenty-one, their livers are perfectly pickled and bursting with flavour. Make sure you pluck the Scouser properly or there'll be bits of curly hair in your paté."

A human mixed grill, with a white man, an Arab, an Asian and a black man – all grilled, with peas, chips, mushrooms, grilled tomatoes and some "ironic black pudding" made with the blood of a pig farmer.

When the aliens arrive to tell us that planet earth is a flake of dry skin on a space-monkey's arse, religion will be finished, and about time to.

I remember the hoo-ha when a British Airways employee was told not to wear a crucifix over her uniform. She stormed out and threatened to sue the airline, which backed down. What bothers me is not BA threatening to sack these people; it's the fact that they gave them a job in the first place.

Here's how you avoid making the same mistake. When interviewing a potential employee, place a bible on the table with half of it sticking out over the edge before inviting them in. Halfway through the interview, "accidentally" knock the bible off the table. If the applicant screams, dives forward and catches that bible like Superman catching a kid thrown from a burning building, it's a "we'll let you know." Anybody who so much as crosses their legs doesn't get the job.

If the candidate is wearing a hat to cover his horns and has a bulge in the back of his trousers where he's tucked his tail into his pants, give him a three-month trial.

If religion really wants to do something constructive, stop telling people they will go to hell if they kill themselves. You're just creating a logjam. Suicidal people are a drain on resources and helping them to live longer just brings everybody else down with them.

Anyone who tries to take their own life and fails should be executed for incompetence. How hard can it be? When people talk about failed suicide attempts they generally write it off as "a cry for help." It is. It's someone crying, "Will someone please help me kill myself because I appear to have fucked it up!"

People must be given grants to kill themselves. This is obviously especially attractive to those with little life insurance. £25,000, to be left to your loved ones after you're gone. We could advertise the service – "The Government – Putting Paid to Misery."

We'll call it the "Lemmings Law." I always thought Lemmings were a real quandary. The kind of courage needed to throw yourself off a cliff was surely more than adequate to deal with any of the challenges life could throw at you. It didn't make any sense.

It now turns out lemmings kill themselves not out of despair or self-hatred but to make room for the younger generation coming through. They put their families before themselves. Exactly what I'm talking about.

Suicide now has such a stigma attached to it the word itself is now being phased out. When my aunt tried to kill herself she was diagnosed not as suicidal, but suffering from AND, or Advanced Negativity Disorder. My aunt attempted closure by washing down three bottles of paracetamol with five gallons of scrumpy, but the scrumpy got her so pissed she threw the tablets up over the bar and landed herself on pubwatch.

Undeterred, auntie fed a hosepipe from her exhaust pipe through the window of her car and started the engine. The car, however, ran on bio-fuel, and after ten minutes she got out of the car with an uncontrollable craving for a sprout butty,

Auntie did eventually succeed in throwing a seven. She shot herself in the head. Unfortunately she used a .44 magnum, which according to Dirty Harry, is the most powerful handgun in the world. It might still be, it might not, and frankly, not being American, I don't fucking care. My aunt put the gun in her ear (!?) and pulled the trigger. The bullet went through her ear, past her eyes so quickly they span round like reels in a fruit machine and out the other ear, killing the old dear sat next to her on the bus.

It was an inglorious end to a glorious pursuit. Auntie's gun was seized by the court, sold, and the proceeds used to clean the bus. She was posthumously convicted of the manslaughter of her fellow passenger, and her ashes thrown over the wall of Wormwood Scrubs.

If people want to commit suicide, give them every help and be done with it. Make it painless, humane and dignified. Build a huge cannon on Dover cliffs and fire suicidal people at France. Being fired out of a cannon will give the AND sufferer an adrenaline rush so strong they'll immediately feel much better and probably change their mind just as they reach Calais, so if they survive the landing they'll be cured – a classic win / win scenario.

Adrenaline therapy is maybe the way forward. Drop suicidal people into war-zones with a rifle and some rations and watch them come home a different person, or bury them with full military honours. How about the French Foreign Legion?

Years ago, when you'd had enough you joined the legion and fought in the desert. It was therapy. If you're going to go, go doing something glorious, like fighting. Don't send the UN into global hotspots, send the Foreign Legion.

People shouldn't have to cut their wrists or string themselves up to achieve closure. It's their life and they should be able to do whatever they want. God, however, won't let them. If you commit suicide you're going to hell, even though Jesus was allowed to give his own life for reasons he considered appropriate. This is preposterous.

The modern Church tries to appeal to the youth of today by appearing more modern when it should be doing the opposite. It was modern civilisation that drove people away from the Church, and more of the same will just make it worse. The Church needs to de-modernise, and quickly.

First up, bring back the crusades. Rally a holy army and set off for the Middle East on the rampage. The youngsters will love it. Fight a holy war, spend the evening feasting, gorging, and copulating, then home to a hero's welcome.

This is how you engage people. This is why we have football hooliganism. When the crusades ceased, football hooliganism developed to fill the void in young men's lives. Football hooliganism is an excellent way for working-class people to let off steam of a weekend. If you ban it, they're only going to find a new avenue for their violent urges. So embrace it; give the hooligans a little bit of wasteland and let them get on with it. Just because it's not your cup of tea.

I myself wanted to be a football hooligan but didn't quite have the right stuff. As I tried to explain to my fellow hooligans during a riot, ripping up your seats and throwing them at the police is all well and good, but what are you going to sit on to watch the second half? You can't sit on the concrete; you'll get piles.

I used to stop in the middle of a fight to check on the score of the game, and giving people Chinese burns didn't seem to work as well as it did on my girlfriend. When I was told to bring some flares to the next game I wore my dad's old trousers.

In the end, the lads just let me tag along because I made them laugh. I held their coats for them whilst they had a barney, and saved their place in the queue if it all went off at half-time.

Of course the crusades and such like are in the distant

past now, but people all over the world still buy into the Muslim versus Infidel bollocks that has continued ever since. If you listen to the far right we all need to be frightened of Muslims now because the Koran speaks of taking up arms to kill Christians. If I was a Muslim, living somewhere around 1265, and 400,000 homosexual white Christians turned up dressed like the Village People, intent on killing every Muslim they found, I think I'd pick up a sword myself. What do you expect them to do? Bend over?

If Muslim radicalism is spreading as quickly as we are led to believe, the Asian community are the ones in real danger. What happens if ninety percent become radicalised and all decide to launch suicide bomb attacks on the same day? The British Asian community could wipe itself out in the space of twenty-four hours.

The second thing the Church needs to do is get back to being scary. People say the Church doesn't connect with people the way it used to, and they're right. What they don't tell you is that the Church used to connect with the people by scaring the living shit out of them; not by inviting them round for a cup of tea and a chat.

People went to Church because they were petrified of the consequences of not going. The rich gave generously and the poor gave their last groat out of sheer, base, naked fear. People are no longer scared of the Church and this is why religion struggles to attract moderate people. Take the word "sacred." Swap the "c" and the "a" and you have "scared." This is no coincidence, and probably the earliest recorded example of subliminal messaging.

Fear will restore the Church's standing. Religion has a colour and its colour is brown. The real genius of the Da Vinci Code was the author's surname.

People will do whatever you want if you get them scared enough, and this is a lesson the Church needs to re-learn. Any bank robber will tell you that the real trick in robbing a bank is to frighten the customers so much you don't actually need to use the gun. You show a dog fear and he'll bite you in the nuts.

Newspapers make millions of pounds frightening their readers to death with exaggerated stories about the end of our way of life. The economy is about to collapse, the Muslims are taking over, the crime wave will soon wash us all away, you're in too much debt, your arse is riddled with cancer etc. And people keep buying the papers because they are worried about missing out on the next great threat. All because of fear.

Excommunication needs to be re-introduced. Holy cops rounding up sinners and torturing them to death before stringing their rotting corpses to Church gates whilst politicians look the other way.

You think they had whip-rounds in the olden days when the Church roof needed mending? Do you think the Church had to beg people for money? No. The Church already had everybody's money because the people were scared of the consequences of not giving. Fix the roof? Just stick a new one on.

People now mainly use Churches as places to get married and have some kind of ceremony to dignify their death, but, as we've already established, there is no dignity in death anymore.

We should just go the whole hog and legalise cannibalism. Burning corpses must be bad for the environment, and sooner or later we are going to run out of room in which to bury people.

The size of the average corpse is also growing. People are taller and fatter than they used to be. You'd be lucky to get twenty stiffs on a plot that would've held twenty-five some thirty years ago. Their bodies take up more space and displace more soil to bury. Where is the soil going?

When your mate dies, don't bury him, don't burn him, and don't bury him at sea; eat him. Don't bring him into Church in a coffin; bring him in on a platter with an apple in his mouth and thirty quid's worth of stuffing up his bum.

When the service is finished, take him to the crematorium and slice a criss-cross pattern on him with a carving knife till he looks like Hellraiser. Rub loads of ginger, thyme and honey into the lacerations and get him in the incinerator. Once he starts to caramelise, quickly whip him out, wrap in foil, and leave for an hour. Then serve him as a big hog roast at the wake. That's how to celebrate somebody's life. Don't remember'em; eat'em. If you died of a heart attack because you were too fat at least let your mates enjoy the crackling.

Cannibalism means no trees are cut down for coffins, nobody goes hungry, and the bones can be used to make furniture or ground down for aggregate. Don't give the bones to your dog because he will just try and bury them, partially destroying the object of the exercise.

With the price of food rocketing and people in the poorer areas of the world starving, cannibalism might be our only hope. This is where the Cannibalism Against Hunger Campaign comes in.

We'll start with pensioners. At the moment we have far too many pensioners. They serve little economic purpose, consume resources willy-nilly and take up too much space, and yet somewhere in the world a child is starving.

Now I have to concede that I find the thought of thousands of pensioners queuing for the abattoir as unacceptable as you. If you frighten them they'll tense up, and the meat will be too tough.

You need to surprise them. Wait for them to leave their house in the morning, watch them walk down the road, then sneak up behind and taser them. Alternatively, employ gamekeepers to take them out from a surrounding hill.

The next time the BBC are filming Last of the Summer Wine trawl the village with a massive fishing net. Arrange a seminar entitled All Modern Comedy is Rubbish, then disguise a big lorry as a town hall. When the pensioners all wander in, shut the lorry up and drive off. Open up launderettes and put superglue on the seats.

We could have rangers, like in the movie, Logan's Run. They can whizz around the streets on those electric buggy things that pensioners drive, but the rangers will have specially tuned ones that can actually go from 0-60, irrespective of how fast it gets there.

This is obviously a controversial idea, and I can understand there being some objections. For a start, pensioners don't have that much meat on them and are hardly the most filling of meals. The only thing they're good for is stew, and the only people who eat stew are pensioners.

Relevant points, but pensioners aren't much good for

anything else. If they're a bit lean, just eat more of them – like little lamb chops. If there isn't enough meat on pensioners, supplement them with more substantial specimens.

Where famine is at its most rampant we'll use bodybuilders. These people are nothing more than gigantic walking steaks. There is more high quality lean meat on a competition standard bodybuilder than a pedigree Aberdeen Angus. If an athlete dies of steroid abuse, stick him in the pot; their hearts are so big they could feed a village.

All the fat from liposuction procedures must also be kept and mixed with the human meat to produce high calorie sausages for the third world. Murderers, paedophiles, drug dealers. Get them in the oven. Now that's a deterrent. Burglars should be kebab-ed. After everything I've said have I stumbled upon an answer to criminality? Could it really be that simple?

Sometimes, when a burglar is convicted of robbing somebody's house, part of the burglars rehab involves going back to the house and having to confront the victims and see the damage and pain they've caused. The victim also gets the chance to confront the burglar, ask them why they did it and maybe understand what drove them to it.

I have a better idea. When somebody has their house burgled and the perpetrator is caught, I want the police to knock at the victim's door with a bag full of chops, sausages, steaks, and black pudding and say, "See these? These were made from the bloke who burgled your house…enjoy."

Some vegetarians point out human's reluctance to eat each other as hypocrisy. Don't get militant about how great meat is and then refuse to eat the same species as you. Let's see how committed you really are.

They have a point, but I differ with them slightly. These vegetarians are suggesting that people should eat humans instead of farmyard animals whereas I would still want to eat animals as well. Roger Rapist would have to taste pretty damn good to stop me eating bacon.

If a pig dies and you leave it there, the other pigs will eat it. Pigs, in other words, are just as keen on bacon as we are. When the farmer's cooking his breakfast in the mornings and the bacon is wafting across the yard, the pigs are out there. "Oi! Smell that everyone! Smell that bacon! Oh boy! Imagine how good that tastes! Oi! Chickens! The reason they smother you in those flashy sauces is because you don't taste of anything!"

That's not their exact words, obviously. Pigs can't speak English, but this is a pretty accurate translation. Can animals communicate? Of course they can. People have pondered in the past (God knows why) if animals are gay. But are they racist? I have long pondered this question, even attempting to write a novel with animal racism as the backdrop.

A snail falls in love with a lady caterpillar, but her family treat him like shit. He's different. They deliberately walk fast at family walks and leave him behind. They put salt on his chips, even though it might kill him. They graffiti his shell when he's asleep.

The snail won't give up, and wins them over by saving a young caterpillar from some young earwig rednecks, though he dies in the process, has a statue erected in his memory, and all the creepy crawlies then live in harmony. How about when national-guard ants had to be called out to escort black ants into redneck red ant schools in Little Rock, Arkansas?

I digress. Recent studies suggest farmyard animals know full well they are being bred for food but accept it as their lot in life, and take pride in being as tasty as they possibly can. Nobody hates a vegetarian as much as a cow.

Cows stand around doing nothing all day, actually helping the farmer to fatten them up. They're happy to do it. If not, they'd be running around that field like Paula Radcliffe. The amount of steroids they're on they could probably run all day if they wanted. Does the farmer come down of a morning to find his cows doing sit-ups, press-ups, running circuits and doing star jumps? No.

Cows are very simple creatures. When the sky turns red and cows lay down, people say it's going to rain. Truth is the cows think the sky is on fire and are lying down to get away from it. Because they're thick.

My cousin had a farm near Hungerford, but decided that the land was too valuable. He sold it to property developers, moved the cows into a shed and made them drink milk all day. He then marketed the milk that came out as twice-refined milk. He called it Double Dairy, and made millions.

Other farmers caught on. My cousin's brother, who, coincidentally, is my cousin as well, had a gardening business. When they won the contract to cut the local parks they saved the cuttings, packaged the grass and sold it to farmers as ready meals for cows. The cows got to eat their favourite meals, indoors, watching Sky Sports News on a giant plasma screen they had fitted to the retaining wall. The milk tasted like silk.

What about all these hippies working on conservation projects, saving the lives of meat eaters that would eat them given half the chance? If they provided the lions and tigers with vegetarian alternatives, and the animals refused to eat them, would they abandon them and leave them to their fate?

Put aside your sensitivity for a moment and think it through. Cannibalism is a good idea. A big dead fat bastard would make the ideal high calorie meal for somebody facing starvation. Anyone whose body fat reaches a certain level should be executed, cooked, frozen, packaged and off they go to the third world. This is not just beneficial to people who are starving, it's also good for the environment.

People now talk about the rising sea levels, but what about dropping land levels? Surely lots of fat people trundling around has a compacting effect on the earth's crust? Heavy people squash things, and as the land gets trampled lower and lower the sea becomes comparatively higher.

Lower land levels means more gap between the planet and the limits of earth's atmosphere, allowing for more swirl, creating greater turbulence, bigger storms and more flooding. The inhabitants of New Orleans spend their days scoffing creole, fried chicken and potato salad; get fat, squash the place lower, Katrina comes along and devastation is the terrible consequence. This is a slightly simplistic explanation, but let's at least take it into consideration.

I remember being kept home from school one day when the infamous Drizzle Derek hit the south coast of England. I went outside to empty my bedpan into the gutter and got really wet. One lady in our street got so wet her underwear got damp and she had to wear two pairs of knickers in one day.

In the days of one service wash a week the lady ran out of underwear by Sunday, and had to go to Church "commando". Exiting the Church she slipped and went head over heels, revealing her growler to a stunned vicar. The locals went mad, chopping all her hair off and chasing her out of town, at least as far as the bus stop, where they made her catch the number 58 to Basingstoke.

The human race has always had an uneasy relationship with water and the sea. So much of the sea is still uncharted or misunderstood, and humans instinctively distrust anything we can't conquer. Now global warming means the sea is threatening to take back the land, and we're frightened. Water is now our enemy.

Some of the water we have on this planet came from outer space. A lot of the water was inside the rock that became our planet, in the form of ice, which came to the surface as steam. A lot of the water on our planet, however, came from meteors. Meteors partly made of ice crashed into our earth, the ice melted, even more water for us.

Maybe the time has come to return some of this water to space. If we can build pipes that can transport oil around the world, we can build a pipe to take water into space. Don't build up from the ground, take the pipe into space and then unfurl it until it reaches earth. It will obviously need to be flame retardant enough not to burn up upon re-entry, but after that, gravity will do the rest.

When the pipe reaches the sea, unplug the end and the vacuum of space will suck the water up from the planet. If Australia is having a mega-drought you can always track round and pump some water down to them. The same can be done with Africa. Why must African nations parch when other countries are disappearing under water?

Why not store the water on Mars? If we develop another

planet with livable conditions we can all spread out a bit. This will also give the fish inadvertently sucked up by the pump somewhere to live and swim about. Don't feel sorry for the fish. It will be an adventure for them. Many humans dream about going into space, these little critters get to go for free.

We can build huge lakes on Mars and use them as fish farms, breeding millions of fish to transport back to earth, directly to the canals going through Africa.

While most of the west seems paranoid about water washing us away, some people just carry on as normal. Why are house builders still building on flood plains? In the hillbilly areas of Montana, wooden lodges are up on stilts so all the bear and cougar shit rolling off the hills passes underneath. In Britain, we should be building houses to the same design so the water will flow under the houses rather than through them.

Houses on stilts will also provide something else; shade. The lack of lovely cool shade created by deforestation is just as important in global warming as the amount of carbon absorbed by the trees themselves. We've exposed the surface of the planet to too much heat, so let's offset this by using compressed land-fill to build synthetic caves where air can cool and chill the planet down a bit.

We also need to start insulating our houses with the stuff they make nappies out of. "Walls absorb the moisture, leaving housey nice and dry." It's a reasonable idea. If the drains are full and overflowing, just make them deeper.

Rising sea levels also bring other dangers. For years, the human race has run the planet in its own interests. We've lived off the land but also the sea as well. The result is species decimated, ecosystems destroyed, and a whole ocean full of creatures out for revenge. When the planet is ninety percent water, we are in a world of shit.

It is a scientific fact that giant killer octopuses evolved from pissed off spiders, washed down the plugholes of human bathrooms. They weren't hurting anybody and didn't mean to end up in the bath, but weren't even given the chance to explain. With a piercing scream, the spider was flushed into the sewers, into the river clinging to a turd and onto the sea, vowing to return one day and level the score.

Take Godzilla. The bloody French test some bombs in a faraway land and the outcome is a giant lizard type, cross-breed, half-reptile, half-serial killer, gallivanting around the civilised world causing all manner of bother. With all the toxic waste going into the rivers in China it could easily happen again.

It wouldn't have to be a Godzilla type creature. Let's face it; a six-foot sea horse would be scary enough. How about a ten-foot ant? A red one who fled your garden years ago after you scalded his entire family with a kettle.

When an ant is bigger than everybody else, does he get cocky, or worried? He's big enough to bully all the other ants and push them around, but in a world where everything is bigger than ants you're still very small, and any anteater is going to make a beeline for the meatiest ant.

What do you do if confronted with a thirty-foot mutated angry worm? You chop him in half and you just get out-flanked by two fifteen-foot-more-mutated-now-even-angrier worms.

There are more disgruntled creatures lurking in the

deep blue sea. What about the maggots? Where do they go? When a fish bites on a fishing line, does he swallow the maggot? When you've got a hook through your mouth and you're being dragged through the roof of your known world the last thing you're thinking is, "Chew that maggot properly or you'll get tummy ache."

Some maggots will be chewed, swallowed, or killed by the hook itself, but some must make it. Where are the maggots going? Are they living at the bottom of the sea like the Water Babies, just waiting for the chance to get even?

What about other mutated sea creatures? A seal the size of a supermarket, or plankton so big whales are being washed up on shore having choked to death on them? Recently, the critics panned the film Mega-Shark versus Giant-Octopus, but I think people need to start taking these it-could-really-happen type films more seriously.

Aged 19, inspired by Jurassic Park, I took a fossilised mosquito I found in my garden and borrowed a frog from next-door 's pond. I took an egg from the fridge, cracked it in half, scoffed the egg and kept the shells. I then stunned the frog, (by telling it Paul McCartney was human and the frogs in the frog chorus were animated) and chucked it in a blender with the mosquito, some protein powder, and some yeast. I then poured the mixture into the eggshell, Sellotaped it together, and left it in the airing cupboard. Ten days later I cracked the egg open, and out jumped an eight-foot long maggot, which jumped out the kitchen window before I could grab it.

Over the next few weeks, farmers began finding cows in trees, having been completely sucked dry, like big furry raisins, and somebody broke into the blood bank and "stole" fifteen pints of blood in one go.

I decided I had to hunt down and kill the beast before anybody found out what I'd done. I took a rotting cow carcass, filled it with Alka-Seltzer, and left it in the garden. When the maggot arrived for his meal the Alka-Seltzer would expand in his belly and pop him like a balloon. Unfortunately the Alka-Seltzer merely cleared up his indigestion, leaving him even hungrier. The maggot was now fifteen-foot long and two-feet across.

The game was afoot. I paid haemophiliacs twenty quid a time to cut their finger and swing on the hammock in our garden, but when the maggot came I couldn't get a clean shot. We lost three good men in one night.

Tracking the beast was proving elusive, and to this day I swear he was being hidden by the badgers (bastards!) One night I pursued him down to the beach where he leapt into the sea. I shot him with harpoons with barrels tied to them, but he still managed to go under, with three barrels on him!

My secret was also out, but it turned out to be my saviour. A local newspaper photographer managed to get a shot of the beast, and the council paid a local bounty hunter called Quint to shoot the thing with a bullet made of pure salt. The creature's existence was blamed on global warming, things went back to normal, and I hung up my lab coat.

Fishes run over by water skiers, crabs displaced from their homes by oilrigs, and the odd killer whale who swam to England and up the Thames one day, only to find himself being molested by hippies in wetsuits. All these creatures are waiting in the sea for us, biding their time.

And what about all the sharks? I almost feel sorry for sharks. I bet when they were young some of them were good fish, but you somehow always knew they were going to turn out bad. "He was such a nice little fish, lovely smile. But you look at the family and he never stood a chance. It's so sad."

When the sea creatures are living off the humans washed into the water they won't be introducing quotas to preserve human stocks, don't you worry about that.

The Environment Police need to address some uncomfortable truths. Can we actually reverse global warming, or is it too late? Surely our money would be better spent exploiting global warming rather than trying to fight it. If this planet is now screwed let's get off it quick. Go with the flow. Why are people not yet living on the moon?

Most of us don't have time to consider these questions and the fact that I do is not something I'm proud of. Like I said, if I had something to occupy my time, be it a career, family, charity work, social life or a pastime I could leave you all in peace. But I haven't.

When I was younger, I was accused of being anally retentive. I'd always thought anally retentive was a posh description for people with constipation and stuffed myself with laxatives...with hilarious consequences. I soon learned the real meaning of the term, and laughed so hard I pooed my pants.

My behaviour first went semi-doo-lally at my seventh-birthday party, when I made all my little friends take a body-fat index test. I then increased or decreased the size of the slice of birthday cake depending or whether or not I felt they could, or were inclined, to burn the calories.

Suffice to say, the line-up for my eighth-birthday party looked like a Paris catwalk, and what a dreadful sight it was.

The advent of size zero models is sick, and reflects a society where moderation and common sense are constantly flattened in the drive for extremism in everything we do.

Women are now killing themselves to look like a pipe cleaner. If men found that kind of shape attractive we could just dig up skeletons from the graveyard and take them out to dinner. The bill would be cheap and afterwards you could skip foreplay with no negative feedback.

Women with fantastic boobs are now losing them as their bodies are stripped of every bit of fat. Have you lost your minds? If men started going to doctors, surgeons, and dieticians and demanding solutions to give them smaller penises women would go mad, and rightly so. We'd be spoiling their fun. Well don't spoil ours.

Without tits the human race would never have prospered and none of us would be here now. When men hunted, they used traps and fishing rods. A woman's breasts were her equivalent. When a man met a woman for the first time his eyes were irresistibly drawn to her breasts. As he looked up, it was hard not to catch her eye, and contact was made, (don't kid yourself it happens the other way round) and the end result at some point was procreation and the spread of the human race.

Do you think kids would be so keen to breastfeed if the milk came out of a woman's elbow?

The magnetism of a woman's fun-bags was something the ancient cultures understood. The Incas didn't lure animals into traps or chase after them with spears; they placed topless maidens at the foot of their temples and waited for the animals to come to them.

When the early Polynesians wanted shark for dinner, they didn't go out fishing. The most buxom woman in the village did some topless sunbathing and lured the sharks towards the shore.

This is why fish stocks are so low and the British fishing industry is dying. Topless sunbathing flourished in this country when people started going on package tours to Spain in the seventies and eighties. People got used to doing it abroad and gradually started to get topless on British beaches. All the fish in the sea were drawn to the coast by the magnetic pull of all those oiled up knockers, meaning more and more were getting caught, to the point where the fish stocks are now almost totally depleted.

This is also why we now have problems with Spanish fishermen trespassing into English waters. Because topless sunbathing took off in Spain first, their fish stocks depleted far quicker than ours, meaning they were forced into British waters to find decent catches. Then topless frivolity came to Britain and the fishing industry found itself squeezed from both sides.

Maybe the Fisheries Ministry should introduce regulations requiring women to face away from the sea when sunbathing topless. I can see some of you are cynical about this theory so let's put it to the test and settle an age-old mystery at the same time.

If you want to catch the Loch Ness Monster, hire Michelle Marsh and Lucy Pinder, and push them out onto the middle of the loch, topless, on lilos. Within five minutes

Nessie won't just have appeared, he'll be doing tricks like a killer whale at Sea World. Him and his brothers, Dessie and Wessie.

That's right. There isn't just one monster, but three. Dessie and Wessie have for years bemoaned the fact that Nessie is the famous one and they have to live in the shadow of the elder brother just because he came along first and was named after the loch. They even changed their names to Dezzy G and Ice Wezzy to look more street, but to no avail.

Minimum breast sizes must be introduced. Any women under a certain size must have compulsory breast enlargements to bring them in line. All boob jobs must be given free on the NHS. Once we lose breasts, like the polar ice caps, we may never get them back.

But size zero is dangerous in so many other ways. A size zero model was killed last year on the London underground after being sucked down a tunnel by the back draft of a departing train. Another perished at London Zoo after being blown between the railings of the tiger cage, and eaten.

The last time I went to the zoo there was a sign outside the piranha pond, giving the time it would take a gaggle of piranhas to strip a human down to a bare skeleton. There were three different estimates; three minutes for a normal person, twenty-five seconds for a super-model, and three days for an American.

That's why piranhas are now an endangered species. When an American kid falls into the river the piranhas tuck in, only for their stomachs to burst half way through. Piranhas are genetically programmed to always finish their meal. Imagine the distress the piranhas must feel as they slowly eat themselves to death, not being able to leave what they can't eat.

Another super-model died after being spun round by the vortex created by a London kerb-cleaning vehicle and fell under a bus. Kensington last year spent nearly one million pounds on altering their drain covers to prevent size-zero models being pushed through the grates by the weight of their expensive hats.

One model I know is so thin she can pick up Sky television just by standing at the top of Streatham Common and raising her right arm in the air. If you look through her right ear you can see Sky Sports News, through her left ear, the Discovery Channel. Sexual harassment charges have also risen sharply on London's buses as commuters press the breasts of super-models, mistaking them for poles with stop buttons.

With global warming and the increase in hurricanes and tornadoes, things will get worse before they get better. The general public will have to put up with size zero women blowing around like tumbleweed, knocking people over, blowing across the road and causing car crashes, getting caught up in overhead pylons and trees, and being blown off cliffs and boats. The emergency services won't know what's hit them.

Anyone below a certain mass must have weights placed in their bag, weighed down like jockeys in a handicap race. The only alternative is to lay some kind of Scalextric track around London, into which the models can be clicked and then glide around the city.

Incidentally, in the future it'll be so windy, sky divers

will stand on the runway, pull their parachutes and be sucked upward with such force that the challenge will be to reach a height of twenty thousand feet, pack your parachute and sky dive through the door of a passing plane.

The only advantage super-light people have is in water. Super-models float better than other people. When the ice caps melt, the planet is flooded and the buildings have washed away, the tallest will be the last to drown, but may find themselves commandeered as canoes by desperate short people.

In areas like Surrey, the super-models go into the country and play poo-sticks, using themselves as poo-sticks. A shark is also less likely to attack a super-model (when they're in the sea, not a Surrey stream,) as they get stuck between their teeth.

When washed away by a flood, fat people are far more likely to drown than thin people; they float just under the surface in the same way dumplings float under the surface of a stew.

Although the concept of a size zero model is disgraceful, the actual models themselves deserve some sympathy. These women are genuinely ill. To deliberately starve yourself to the point Geldof is organising concerts in your garden…well. Many of the models themselves are really nice people.

For example, I read an article by a super-model pressure group trying to confront the problem of ugly people. Apparently they're bad for morale. As part of an initiative to put something back into society, the models had suggested donating ten percent of their fees from London Fashion Week towards paying for ugly people to get plastic surgery and liposuction.

The article went on: "Growing a second chin to give your girlfriend something to hang on to during sex may seem like a remarkably sweet gesture, but the novelty soon wears off."

They're missing the point. The benefits of a double chin far outweigh the downsides. Having a DC means you don't have to bother with a scarf in winter. If you fall asleep in a restaurant your chin stops your head falling forward on to your chest. A DC is your life support machine if you ever find yourself the survivor of a plane crash and people are starving.

When you really want to remember something, get somebody to write it on your spare chin in biro. Boxers are encouraged to develop their chin baggage to help absorb the force of their opponent's punches. If your health freak wife tries to stop you eating chocolate, hide a Star Bar under your chin. Tests have shown that people who come off their motorbikes have a greater chance of survival if they have a double-bubble – it fills up the space between their head and the inside of their helmet, reducing "rattle-around-age."

If you're stressed, don't jiggle balls around in your hand; play with your chin. If you need inspiration, stroke your chin the way a musketeer would stroke his goatee beard. An old friend of mine, Randy Crabtree III, had the biggest DC I'd ever seen, and yes, he was a Yank. When Randy was drinking in bars he'd beat his double chin like Tarzan every time he saw a woman he fancied, and claims it, "Never failed to get me laid."

I regularly visit my doctor for lipo-injections. Once the hoover is full up with other people's cheeseburger residue, I go round and get it injected in. "Doctor, quick, I keep losing weight, I can feel myself getting all shallow and superficial, sort me out."

The only downside is the Japanese, who've apparently promised Greenpeace they'll stop whaling if they can have permission to harpoon fat swimmers instead.

But then it struck me; the super-models might be onto something, at least as far as other women are concerned, for this simple reason. Ugly women have nice personalities. If you then give them loads of plastic surgery they will then become lush, and therefore the perfect woman. This will have two main benefits:

One. The years of being ignored or teased about their looks will now be seen as a character-building time, when a personality was forged, they saw the other side of life and were left alone to concentrate on their education. Is it a coincidence that women who blossom later in life are nicer than those who were beautiful from the get-go?

Two. Bullying and teasing will stop. Who wants to risk offending an easy target when years later they get made really beautiful and you've blown your chance of some Essex Yoga?

Maybe kids should be allocated to schools with students who reflect their looks, as well as their intelligence. There will be schools for ugly intelligent kids, good looking thick kids, beautiful intelligent kids, and one for the thick ugly ones, complete with razor wire, armed guards, and a chemical experimentation wing.

Is it wrong to look at eleven-year-old kids and rate them according to looks and sexual desirability? Probably.

I would like to make an important point here. If people want to have plastic surgery then let them have it. But let's not force ugly people into having a procedure. Ugly people do have their uses. Our local council employs ugly people to stand by the side of the road just before accident black spots or dangerous bends. The cars reduce their speed to gawp at shovelhead and are less likely to have a crash.

Other ugly people make livings as scarecrows on organic

farms after the crows sussed the straw variety. On normal intensive farms this is not necessary as the pesticides make the crops taste rank. It wasn't until this the crows realised they weren't actually meant to eat the corn. Until then, many thought the scarecrows were farmers holding their arms out as a welcoming gesture.

When the farmers started spraying the crops with chemicals, the crows went to the farmers' houses to complain about the food and how downhill it had gone. An ear bashing and volley of buckshot soon cleared the confusion up.

Fat bloke in my local pub has a story about Bill Gates, which he swears is true. Fat bloke reckons Bill Gates, as a teenager, was sick of his nerdy looks but was petrified of plastic surgery, so he set out to become so rich he could pay for everybody in the whole world to have laser eye surgery to make him appear good-looking. If this is true, he's probably made enough, and proves that vanity and the desire to make money can achieve so much more than honesty and love.

Now most people will tell you plastic surgery needs to be carefully regulated. The body also can only take so much. It's important that people can handle the process psychologically, and have realistic expectations.

Nonsense. Just let them get on with it. In fact, encourage the nutters to go berserk and have all kinds of stuff done. They enjoy the ridicule; it's a form of masochism.

If Michael Jackson's nose couldn't take any more surgery they should've given him a second one, leaving him free to continue his love of plastic surgery whilst preserving what was left of his original hooter. If he was worried about looking weird, he could've joined the noses with a bar running between the two, in what's known as a catamaran nose job.

You could get your nose turned upside down. If you work in a sewage farm or with noxious substances it would reduce the amount of fumes entering your nose, and if you're a carpenter it'll give you somewhere to put your pencil while you're measuring up.

Just go for it. Give women fanny tightening procedures so severe you'd need a titanium condom and a ten-yard run up just to get some purchase.

The government should see the potential that comes with a good-looking country. If everybody was good looking and sexy, all sex would be great and everybody would go to work feeling fulfilled and de-stressed. If everybody you see is as beautiful as your ex, the end of a relationship need no longer be a big deal; just get yourself an equivalent model.

Surely the whole point of a meritocracy is that everybody who goes for a job is judged on their ability, whereas many candidates (women in particular) are employed for their looks. If everybody were super-shagtastic you'd have a level playing field.

Would I draw the line somewhere? Yes I would. Botox injections. Botox is a poison that paralyses the muscles under your skin, meaning they can't move or twitch, and your skin doesn't wrinkle. And people pay money to have it done. A good hard punch in the face will get the same results, and compress down the blubber on your cheeks as well.

People now injecting themselves with paralyzing poison

to avoid some wrinkles. What happens if your body becomes addicted to the poison? So much so it starts to manufacture its own? You'll wake up one morning and not be able to move. Your entire body will be as smooth as a bar of soap, and about as much use.

What's the next great cosmetic innovation? "We injected this person with anthrax in order to cure her knobbly knees, whilst this patient over here had small-pox injected into her tits to stop them sagging."

Can you imagine anything more tragic than a turkey getting botox injections in December to fix their scraggy chin and wattle because they want to look their best for the festive season?

Some problems are irreversible. Kids, for example, are not just getting fat; they're being born twice the size as well. Can the planet take the increase in weight? In twenty-five-years time all babies will be born by caesarean section and we'll need modified kerb-lifting machines to take them out.

Many women are already having caesareans when they don't need to. These women are said to be "too posh to push." Rich women in Los Angeles who intend to have lots of kids are now having large zips fitted to their bellies so they can be opened up like a pencil case.

How big are we going to be in fifty years? Planes with two sets of wings, and boats with water-wings on. Tidal waves the size of Berkshire hitting New York as fifty thousand fat fucking holidaymakers simultaneously jump into the sea off Newquay. Jesus Christ, jump in softly can you?

When such a day arrives, all women will be "too posh to push" or "not stupid enough to try and naturally deliver a baby that weighs more than they do." Any woman who even attempts a natural birth will end up with a front bottom like Ilfracombe Harbour.

The women that give birth to these babies must have legs like Bulgarian power-lifters. Professional female athletes will be getting pregnant by large men just because carrying the baby around for nine months is better than three months altitude training. Imagine the spring in your step once you've had that thing out of your belly.

Some of these babies are two-foot long for Christ's sake. Did they have their legs tucked behind their head? That tickling sensation in the back of mum's throat in the weeks before she gave birth was the baby's arm. If these kids get any longer their legs will be hanging out, leaving parents buying their kids socks and shoes weeks before they're born. These kids can eat eight mashed bananas in one sitting. It's no wonder the price of fruit has gone up.

With massive babies, Aids, STDs, low hanging vulva, men claiming to be on the male pill, thrush, internet porn meaning men want at least fifteen positions per bunk-up with a cream-pie shot at the end, cystitis, post natal depression, which hairstyle they should be sporting – be it a Brazilian or a Beckham, thongs, panty pads, clit piercing, double penetrations and people singing "whoooaaa Bodyform!" Women could be forgiven for thinking World War Three has been declared on their fanny. When celebrities like Madonna are pictured running through the park they normally have two bodyguards with them – one to protect her, and one to protect her house of fun.

The good news is that I, once more, have invented a solution that could make me even more money than the

Snot-hoover™. Outside banks, the most valuable things in society are normally stored in museums, who use sophisticated laser systems to protect them. We've all seen them in films – St Trinian's, Ali G Indahouse, The Wrong Trousers, and Entrapment. What we need are the Laing patented Big Sister™ laser pads, with adhesive backing, that can be stuck to the inside of women's thighs whilst they are asleep. These laser pads can then generate a laser field to guard a woman's HQ until the morning, where, no doubt, a new threat awaits.

What about the impact on the world of sport? (Of mega-large babies.) Even if the human race keeps getting bigger and bigger, stronger and stronger, faster and faster, surely we'll reach a stage where the world 100 metres record can't be broken.

Every day we witness the battle between the Irish and the Arabs to build and run the best stud farms and breeding operations to dominate the world of horse racing. They are missing the real opportunity. When I make my money I intend to start stud farms for human athletes.

Retired athletes will be bred like racehorses, according to their bloodlines. Olympic champions will be sold for breeding and put out to stud, and if that isn't an incentive to become an Olympic athlete, I'd like to know what is. Olympic sperm will be bought and traded like frankincense. When Usain Bolt finally runs a sub-nine-second 100m he'll have a kid waiting for him with a bottle of Lucozade, a fit bird with some flowers, and one of my stable hands with a copy of Playboy, some baby oil and a test-tube.

Stuff the medals and the glory, think of the retirement. Days spent running around a lovely green paddock, fresh hay to sleep in every night, all your meals provided, and once a week some lovely athletic young female brought in for you to impregnate. I'll even supply a stable-hand to grab your old tadger and guide it in for you.

People's family trees will be traced and documented to look for the right genes and pedigree to excel in the sporting arena. Most people, by then, will know their family trees as a result of the modern craze for researching your heritage. If I could, I don't think I'd bother. Do you really want to know that your uncle was a Nazi, your great grandad was a transvestite, and your great auntie was a prostitute?

I said, "If I could," just then because, in reality, I can't. The early years of my life are a mystery. I was raised in the New Forest by a pack of wild mink that had been released from the local farm by animal rights activists.

At the age of five a kindly fox offered to escort me to the nearest man-village, where I was taken in by a couple of lesbians and raised in a commune near Brockenhurst. To be fair, they let me go to a mainstream state school and tried to give me a balanced upbringing, though things didn't go smoothly.

I was thrown out of the school nativity play after a dispute over image rights, and banned from playing kiss chase for kissing the wrong end. I later received a life ban from rounders after I led my team from the field after allegations of ball tampering.

The school I went to was so rough we lost our free milk years before the other schools when the kids started using the bottles to make Molotov cocktails. The shop across the road used to sell fake snot bubbles to hang out of your nose. Every morning, if you hadn't managed to generate a real snot bubble by the time you got to school you had to go in and buy one or you'd get beaten up for being a snob.

My secondary school days didn't fare much better. I began with an ill-fated attempt to assassinate the head prefect with a "dirty" custard bomb, followed by a brief suspension after I kidnapped my RE teacher on suspicion of Christian fundamentalism.

On my thirteenth birthday, the two lezzingtons lost patience and traded me for a bong and a goat to a fisherman from Mevagissey, where I worked mending nets. The dad I've referred to so far in this book was actually my step-dad. He was very busy and times were hard so little time was spent in port, meaning I was required to maintain the nets whilst they were actually being used.

Can you imagine anything more heartbreaking than being underwater, fixing nets as the fish put their little fishy faces up against the mesh, shouting, "Give us a break mister, just let us go this once, they won't miss little old me. I've got four kids to feed."

If evolution is such a wonderful thing, why haven't fish evolved that can chew through nets? Try telling the cod that are facing extinction that there's nothing to worry about because evolution will save the day. If fish had razor sharp teeth they could chew through the nets and escape.

Why haven't fish evolved to taste disgusting to humans? If fish tasted so bad it made us physically sick we'd stop catching them. If fish could emit an odour, a bit like a skunk, they could repel humans who were tempted to even try eating them.

There is prophecy amongst fish, about "The One." A fish born inside the nets, that can pass through them at will, chewing them up with his razor sharp teeth. He alone will vanquish the fishing industry, and rescue the cod stocks from extinction.

Inspired by this prophecy, I'm presently working on a screenplay about a fish that can chew through nets. Pixar or Dreamworks will obviously be keen to option the story, which features a young fish, mocked as a kid for having huge teeth, much in the same way Dumbo was for having large ears, until he gets older and starts tearing around the sea, chewing up nets and rescuing fish like Superman, or Superfish. I've called it Guppy the Gobby Cod Razor Teeth Saviour and the curse of the Muslim Fundamentalist Octopus.

Without wanting to give too much away, by the end of the movie, he's halted global warming, saved the seals, the dolphins and the coral reefs, negotiated an end to fishing with the EU, started his own sea-salt export business, built a new mosque for the Muslim octopi, and Lois Lanefish is firing out spawn like a generator at a foam party.

Don't worry. If fish start chewing nets up, the humans will still get their fish. The sea will eventually become overcrowded and you'll be able to walk up to the quayside and simply scoop some fish out in a metal bucket, but watch your fingers. Voila. A ready supply of fresh lean fish, without the hassle of risking life and limb to go out and catch it.

Commercial fishing would therefore die out, leaving the fishermen free to pursue lucrative salvage careers or tourism fishing.

Roughly 250,000 boats or something lay at the bottom of the North Atlantic alone. All those wrecks are not only polluting the sea, they are raising sea levels. Take all the wrecks, coral, and shot-down planes out of the sea and global sea levels will drop back down to a reasonable level.

This is an important point. The reason sea levels keep rising is because we keep putting more and more in the seas, displacing water upward. You could drop ocean levels by a foot just by grounding every single submarine on the planet.

Every oilrig, boat or tanker that ploughs through the shipping lanes, every single pier, underwater research team or marine biologist is displacing water and flooding our planet.

"Everybody out of the water now!"

Aged twenty-one, I resigned my net mending job, citing lack of oxygen, and moved to Newbury, where I got a job as a freelance speed bump. It was okay at first, but the kids in the cars got fatter and fatter, and people started driving heavy four-by-four vehicles to compensate for the bumping and suspension damage. It got a bit much.

The one thing I learned about speed bumps is that most people speed up when they see one rather than slow down. They pull into the middle of the road to even out the effect of the bumps and swerve into busy bus stops in the process. Literally tens of people have taken to flying long journeys rather than driving because they can't face the speed bumps, increasing global warming.

As a result I have decided to announce the formation of my new pressure group, Caucasian Men Against Speed Bumps. I've specified Caucasian because I feel that an ethnic element will give it that extra oomph.

Personally, and I think I speak for everybody here, I

would rather run over an away team from the local Derby & Joan club at 33 mph and spend fifteen years in prison than have to go over another frigging speed bump.

We…do not…need…speed bumps. Let me tell you the main cause of people getting run over in this country. Don't tell anybody, but it's people running out in front of cars without looking. Of course you can't say it because it's insensitive, so we look for somebody to blame because that's how intelligent societies work.

Years ago, when you got run over, the driver used to get out, put you over his knee and smack your bum for getting in his way. When I was run over by an ice cream van, aged six, Luigi stuck the van in reverse and ran over me again for spilling his hundreds and thousands. In other words it was my fault for running into the road.

It was no big deal. We did something about it. We had the Green Cross Code Man. Where did he go? Approaching little children, telling them to look both ways, and reminding us he wouldn't always be there when we crossed the road.

He had to go of course. Parents understandably weren't keen on a grown man running around in a Spandex suit and cape, grinding his lunchbox into the backs of young children as they waited to cross the road.

But it worked! Up and down the country, kids were stood at the side of the road, saying, "Look left and right. Look left again. Do it properly or you'll have that cunt off the tele down here."

I know there was less traffic in those days, but less congestion meant cars could go much faster; if you hit a kid in those days you'd absolutely splatter it.

So let's bring back the Green Cross Code Man, dig up

the speed bumps, and if a kid gets run over, leave him there for a few hours until it sinks in that roads are dangerous, then send him to bed with no dinner. If a kid gets run over twice, send him to prison. It'll give him time to consider the damage to people's cars he's caused in an environment where there are no roads or traffic.

If the kids continue to get bigger all of this will be irrelevant. The cars will be in more danger than the pedestrians. Whole families killed after the driver lost control going round a corner and wrapped the car around a fifteen-year-old rugby player.

As I stated a minute ago, all women will soon have caesareans because the kids will be too big, but it's not only women who can have caesareans. Men can as well, and I've had one.

My ex-girlfriend belonged to a strange semi-Calvinist religious sect. When we decided to start a family, my girlfriend said although she was happy to have my child, she didn't want to have to go through the messy experience of sex to get pregnant. Masturbation was also immoral, so she opted for a "caesarean conception".

This is why I have only one testicle. In caesarean conceptions the man's scrotum is cut open, and a testicle removed. There are various ways of harvesting the sperm – my surgeon opted for the "crush a grape" method. With my girlfriend laid out on a bed, the minister held my testicle over her belly and squeezed it until the sperm oozed out and into her stomach via her belly button.

I have to admit to being unconvinced about the whole deal, but within two weeks my girlfriend was pregnant. My testicle, however, died before they could re-attach it. I took it home and put it in a glass case in the hall. Eight months later, my heavily pregnant partner wandered downstairs in the middle of the night, thought it was one of the aliens from the movie Mars Attacks! and fainted. The testicle is now in the loft.

My scepticism over the baby's conception was justified when the baby was born. A healthy young boy, eight pounds in weight and as black as a newly laid road.

I confronted my girlfriend. She said it was no big deal and that millions of white women have black babies now. These kids were known as "rainbow babies," and seen as a symbol of hope. When I pointed out that both of us were white she accused me of racism and assured me that Winston Exodus Junior was definitely mine.

At first I took it quite hard, not knowing what to do for the best. He was a lovely kid, and the first time he looked at me and burbled, "Daddy" I knew I couldn't desert him. I had responsibilities and needed to knuckle down. It was easier than I'd anticipated, and as time went by I found that being the father of a black child in a rural area had its benefits.

I found myself invited to all sorts of shindigs in the local black community and made lots of new friends. I learned to look at things from a different perspective and talk with people who'd, despite the prejudice and difficulties they'd experienced, kept their spirit, hopes and fantastic sense of humour.

In addition to this, the local chapter of the Klu Klux Klan were surprisingly sympathetic. Indeed, after much heated debate, they agreed to let me continue my membership on a month-by-month basis, subject to review.

During the week I followed my usual routine of Klan

meetings, the odd rally, playing pool at the Grand Wizard's social club, and cake baking on a Thursday. At weekends, it was reggae parties, domino tournaments, cricket matches and Red Stripe lager.

When a Jamaican Yardie pulled a gun on me outside the chip shop the Klan ran him out of town, and when the redneck next to me refused to cut back his tree when it grew over my fence, the Nation of Islam went round and kicked the granny out of him.

I decided to work to bring the two communities together. I would work to moderate the Klan and dilute its rather harsh message, and work with the black community to help them integrate more.

Co-existence is the key. You don't have to live in each other's pockets and patronise each other with half-hearted integration policies and empty platitudes to be happy. If you can live side-by-side in an atmosphere of mutual respect, then that will do.

My new black mates called me a honky and a white cunt, and I called them spear-chuckers. My Klan mates called me "Black Magic" because of my magic sperm that produced black babies and I called them honky redneck trailer trash...and everyone lived happily ever after.

It didn't last long. One evening the Klan came round to pick me up for a rally just as some Black Panthers stopped by to return my copy of Lara Croft – Tomb Raider. A week before, one of my Klan buddies had asked to borrow the game. I said that I'd lent it to my brother, but he could have it afterwards. He hadn't realised that by "brother" I meant Desmond X.

Now everybody was angry. My Klan mate was not happy

knowing a black man had got to play Lara Croft before him, and the leader of the local Panthers, the Honourable Elijah Aswad King, berated the Panthers for playing a computer game based on a rich, imperialist, white bitch.

My black friends in the domino club were not impressed to know I was still in the Klan. Things were a bit sensitive at the time, after the local white supremacist team had turned up the previous week with white dominos with white spots on. The match was a farce. As a punishment, I was dropped from the team for a match against South Reading Nomads. We lost the tie and I was blamed.

Banished from both my communities I sought refuge in the Asian quarter. Lonely and isolated, I allowed myself to become radicalised by some local militants, changed my name to Abdul Kareem Mohamed, and tried to blow up the local Christian Aid bookstore with a box of out of date fireworks. When the heat closed in I left my family and went on the run.

What's the lesson in all of this? It's hard to say. A part of me still blames Lara Croft for the whole saga, but maybe I'm just looking for a scapegoat. Integration is hard and nobody comes out of these situations with any credit. Prejudice is a feature of every society, whether black, white, Asian, Arab, Christian, or Muslim, and everybody has committed atrocities in their history. Nobody has a clean slate or the right to preach and maybe if we all acknowledged the fact once and for all we could all move forward and live in harmony.

If we can't live in harmony then sooner or later we'll just have to partition the world. Europe for the white people, Africa for the blacks, Asia for the Asians, the Far East for the Orientals, and New Zealand for the Australians....all right, all right, calm down it was just a fucking joke.

Is that a racist idea, or just blatant common sense? Let's make all immigration or migration illegal. If your country is crap just make it better, don't leave. The Berlin Wall was eventually knocked down, but if East Germany had been a nice place to live it would still exist. Or we could just have another war, though one in which not too many people die.

Future wars will focus more on utilising technology to disrupt electricity, communications, transport links, and disabling army facilities rather than destroying them. Friendly fire will soon be the main cause of casualties in war. Allied troops are now trained to run into battle backwards on the basis they're in more danger from their own side than the enemy.

With the growth in technology now moving faster than Usain Bolt's underpants, wars will become ever more common and regular. The casualties will soon be so small war will be seen as a cleaner, safer solution than politics. Winning a war means you can impose your will on another country rather than waste years arguing pointlessly in large supra-national organisations.

Those dastardly Iraqis used to put families and westerners in front of military targets to prevent them being attacked. They were known as human shields. In this country we take the opposite view, putting d-list celebrities in front of places we'd like to see bombed.

What casualties we did take in Iraq were due to health & safety weenies making the army wear high-viz bibs. Fitting reversing sensors and "vehicle reversing" voiceovers to tanks meant they crashed less but kept giving the game away on night missions.

The average anti-war protester needs to show more restraint and think their ideas through a bit more clearly. As for the posh students; mass produced rich kids, all sitting on the pavement banging on about how deep they are, and how *so* against the war they are.

"Oh my God, like, I'm home from Uni? Where I just get so hammered? And then I like, went to Uni again the next day, and like, did bugger all work? And then got hammered? And like, Uni's so cool? And then I like, got hammered again? Oh-my-God, I like, so hate the war?" To these kids Iraq is something you stretch poor people out on when they haven't paid their taxes.

It gets worse. Parents dragging their kids onto the streets to speak up for mummy and daddy's "causes." You know as well as I do, you can get whatever response you want from a nine-year-old kid, depending on how you phrase the question.

You explain to a nine-year-old kid that war is bad they'll say, "Yes, mummy/daddy" and join your protest. If you explain to the same kid that wars are necessary, they'll happily follow you on a pro-war march. You ask the average nine-year-old war protester what they also stand for they'll probably say free chocolate for everybody and the abolition of school, but you wouldn't give it to them.

Instead of constantly criticising the negative elements of war, we should learn to embrace the benefits. War is technology's answer to natural selection. It's survival of the most advanced. Many advances in human history have started out as military projects, such as fondu kits, hair gel or mittens with a piece of string connecting them. The mittens were invented to allow commandos to abseil down cable-car runs when in the Alps, or trip up Japs in the jungle. The mother of all invention is not necessity; it's survival.

Maybe the time has come to be done with it, and declare World War Three officially open. Get the Queen to do a speech and cut a ribbon, and then find out the hard way, once and for all, whose side God really is on.

Whatever the original intentions, religion has, and continues, to get millions of innocent people killed. If Jesus does ever come back, he'll probably be arrested and detained for incitement to violence. What if Jesus came back, but accidentally materialised in Iran? What if Allah came back and ended up in Alabama, or Massachusetts?

Of course the greatest threat to organised religion is the supernatural. People tell their kids there's no such thing as aliens, monsters or ghosts, but the very same people will then go to Church on a Sunday when there's a lot more proof that ghosts exist than God.

I had a ghost once. Was I frightened? Not really. Most ghosts are very placid and nothing to be afraid of. Most people think ghosts are the spirits of people who died horrible deaths or died with unfinished business, who roam the spirit world looking for closure, so they can pass to the other side. These ghosts do exist, but there are others.

Some people die when they are not meant to and remain in limbo. Some ghosts are created when the spirit has purpose for them and gives them the option of staying in the spirit world for a bit. Some ghosts, however, die comical deaths and are simply too embarrassed to move on.

There are numerous examples. Like the hunter who shot

a deer on the ledge above him, only for the deer to fall off the ledge and land on him.

My ghost died when he was practising for a pancake-flipping contest. Alone in his kitchen he made an ultra-thick pancake so it could handle lots of practice flips. Once in the garden, he flung the pancake skyward with such force he staggered backwards and knocked himself unconscious on his bird-table. As he lay flat on his back the pancake came down, landed on his face, and suffocated him.

He wasn't much better as a ghost. He'd write messages on the wall in blood, but would always try to be too ambitious. I'd come downstairs in the morning, try to enter my front room, only to be greeted with screams.

"Noooooooo! Don't come in yet! It's not ready! Don't look!"

"Oh no....Let me in."

"I'm not finished. It's a message in blood for you!"

"Why is there two pound on the stairs?"

"Well, I run out of blood, so I used the tomato ketchup. That's for you to buy a new jar."

"Jesus Christ! If you weren't already dead..."

I couldn't turn the lights out at night because he was afraid of the dark, and couldn't see what he was doing. He tried to pass through the wall one day, and to be fair he was fifty percent successful. Having passed into the wall cavity he couldn't get out the other side. I had to get the builders round to rip out the plasterboard and let him out.

After that, he wouldn't go through walls anymore. He used to ring me up at work to tell me he was locked out. I had to get a cat flap fitted to the front door for him to squeeze through; a situation that sufficed until a gang of very small Kosovans broke in and stole my George Foreman Lean Mean Grilling Machine.

In the end I decided I'd had enough, and flushed him down the toilet.

Not all ghosts are a liability. I know of a removal firm in Derbyshire that use poltergeists to move particularly heavy furniture, and ghosts would make excellent security guards.

Fortune telling is also under-utilised. A gypsy friend of mine made a fortune by reading the gussets of men's underpants. Not clean from the washing machine, but after a day's wear. As my friend put it, "You can tell a lot more about a bloke from the state of his pants than you can from the palm of a hand."

Unfortunately, my friend also specialised in the "near future" i.e. she wasn't able to tell the future past the coming fortnight. If her prediction hadn't come true in two weeks, it wasn't going to. She was giving back 90% of her fees in refunds – classic short-term strategy. Disillusioned, she quit and took a job renovating the shells of large dead tortoises and selling them on to smaller upwardly mobile tortoises.

Curb your cynicism. When I rang the producers of the Harry Potter movies I was assured that no special effects were used at any time. Everything was real. Of course they had to keep this a secret, because if people had found out that Voldemort really was back they'd have freaked, and the hospitals of Britain would've been jam-packed with kids with split heads from trying to find platform nine and a half.

Reverse negative energy flow and release the supernatural. Murder could all but be wiped out. If the victim could come back and name the killer, wouldn't that make a potential killer think twice?

You're obviously relying on the ghost to be honest. Is he grassing up the right person, or is he exploiting the situation to settle an old score and get someone else banged up for his death? There's no such thing as a perfect solution to crime, as Tom Cruise found out in Minority Report.

There's only one snag with the supernatural – exorcists. This is an industry that does more harm than good and needs stricter regulation, after all, possession is nine tenths of the law. Exorcising souls is one thing but where does the demon go afterwards? It's a bit like ASBOs; throwing them out is one thing, but all they're going to do is go off and bother somebody else.

My research shows that it is actually feasible to build containment units, just like the Ghostbusters. And there's always Azkaban prison.

Prisons? I hear you say. He's spoken at length about law and order, but didn't ask whether or not we should lock more people up. Of course we should lock them up, the more the better. If I were Prime Minister I'd build prisons seventeen miles high and seventy miles square if I had to. I'd also lower the age at which you can jail a kid to eight. On the way to prison I'd get the van to drive through a ghost train to really shit them up.

Some say you shouldn't put people in prison because it encourages villains to mix with other criminals. What do you think they're doing on the fucking outside! You seriously think the average criminal hates prison because it takes him away from his healthy social network and into one that will lead him into trouble?

"Oh, Josh, you simply must get me out of here! It's full of villains! I should be at book club tonight, and we were meant to be doing Crime and Punishment this week! Oh, the bitter irony!"

No soup kitchens are going to be a man short, no old ladies will be struggling across the road unaided, and no previously tight family units will be struggling whilst druggy-pants is in nick. Even criminals, deep down, know they deserve it. When a criminal commits a crime he knows the risk he's taking, and prison is the criminal equivalent of winning Dusty Bin.

Keeping people out of prison is the brainchild of ivory tower intellectuals, lowered into council estates in large shark cages, to study working-class people in their natural environment. Occasionally they'll tranquillise a local, to study its teeth and droppings. They don't need to tag them, as most of them have already got tags courtesy of the courts.

Am I being too harsh? Maybe, but it's an unfortunate fact that people with good intentions frequently do more damage than people deliberately trying to make things worse.

Health & safety at work might have seemed a good idea up to a point, but it's gone too far. I crashed my car into a building site once, and instinctively aimed for the worker in the high-viz bib because he was the first thing that caught my eye.

People being killed at work used to be seen as a form of natural selection. When a big hole collapsed burying a gang of navvies, it was seen as a cheap convenient funeral for people who were going to die soon anyway.

If the workplace provided a venue for the reckless and

dopey to kill themselves it wasn't necessarily a bad thing. If you kept them alive at work they would only go into the wider world and do something dangerous, and probably kill somebody else into the bargain.

Danger is good. Danger is healthy. It weeds out the weak and daft. As Hollywood has continuously shown us, nothing reunites dysfunctional splintered families more than being chased through the jungle by dinosaurs, running from aliens, or having your son kidnapped. As Detective John McClane proved, saving your estranged wife from terrorists is a great way to mend a relationship, though John's obsessive-compulsive personality and drinking inevitably screw things up once again.

I have to say that Holly McClane/Gennaro must go down as one of the more ungrateful characters in modern cinema history. She clears off to LA with the kids for a new job, leaving her husband behind, who then saves her life not once, but twice. By the third film, however, he's alone again.

I know, I know, we don't know what goes on behind closed doors. John probably does very little housework, doesn't make enough time for family commitments and always brings his work home with him. He never cuts the grass when he says he's going to, misses the bin collection because he's got a hangover, and is heavy handed in dealing with issues with the kids. But give the guy a break; at least he's not boring.

The people I feel sorry for are the villains. Hans Gruber and General Esperanza could be sat on a beach now earning twenty percent, but instead had to die for the sake of a relationship that was doomed to failure.

Men in films constantly risk their all for love and you have to ask yourself why. Indiana Jones can't hold a relationship down for long, James Bond seems to have real trouble with commitment, and I'd be very surprised if Han Solo and Princess Leia lived happily ever after.

Time and time again I failed in my efforts to contact George Lucas with my plans to develop the Star Wars saga past episode 6. Stars Wars – Episode 7 – Luke Gets in With the Bad Crowd.

Luke and Leia now rule the universe, but Luke is rapidly bored with debates on sexism, taxation, expenses scandals and galaxy warming. After the euphoria of the downfall of the Empire has worn off, people rapidly lose patience, and, like Winston Churchill after World War Two, Luke finds himself forced out of government. He becomes bitter and twisted, succumbs to the dark side, and the whole sorry business begins again.

The Millennium Falcon fails its MOT on emissions, and has to be converted to bio-fuel. Han Solo's drinking spirals out of control and puts him in rehab, triggering a bitter custody battle with Leia over their son, Duke, who goes to spend the weekend with Uncle Luke and comes back with red eyes and a real attitude problem.

I don't want to divulge any more details, as I want to leave you wanting more. Lucas has now sold Star Wars to Disney. Maybe I can get more sense out of them.

Anyway, health & safety is not the only example of do-gooders making people's lives worse. Volunteer work must be outlawed and charities abolished.

Charities undermine the achievements of underprivileged people. By giving money and resources the charities are ensuring that the UMAC, or Upwardly Mobile Aspiration Centre, will never be given the credit they deserve for their achievements.

A charity shop in Newbury recently had a sign in the window saying, "Sale Now On." I couldn't believe it. When was the last time you saw charity shop customers standing outside the shop muttering, "Yeah, yeah, they've got some really nice stuff in that charity shop, but I'm not paying those prices. I'll wait till the sale."

Charity is not about giving as little as possible. A charity shop sale should involve doubling the prices, so that people, for a limited time, can give even more money to charity. Are they having sales because they have a new line coming and want to shift last season's ranges?

I entered the shop and dispensed a volley of home truths, the word "fuck" helping to give my arguments extra clarity. Constables were summoned, and I hastily retreated.

When I was wasteful, my fisherman foster father used to ask me if I thought money grew on trees. I thought he was giving me a clue, and used to spend hours roaming orchards and forests in search of that special branch. As you grow older you learn to appreciate the value of money, and how generosity, philanthropy, and giving money to charity are traps only the stupid fall into.

My foster father used to drum this into me. He used to say, "If you see a man drowning, put your foot on top of his head," a lesson that cost me my life-saving certificate and my dad very nearly his life when he fell overboard one day.

When Paula Radcliffe is winning a marathon, she doesn't stop half-way through, go to the back and start helping the runners that are struggling. This is very much like life. Have you not seen Saving Private Ryan?

People give to charities because they feel they are doing a good deed and that good people get their just deserts in life. What goes around comes around. Well it doesn't.

What goes around does not come around. There are plenty of corrupt thieving bastards that have lived successful lives, surrounded by decadence, fame and wealth. Robert Maxwell died, but only very, very late in life. He'd had his fun and was probably happy to check out when he did to avoid the shit-storm headed his way.

In order to be accurate the saying needs "eventually" added to it. What goes around comes around...eventually. You'll lead a life of corruption, decadence and depravity. You'll shaft pensioners, the Inland Revenue, even your own friends and family. You'll sleep with beautiful woman, drink fine wines, eat in the best restaurants and watch concerts and sports matches from the best seat, but later on you'll die and everybody will hate you...eventually.

Have everything in life you wanted and be hated after your death? Most people would take that, especially the disillusioned fifty-somethings who never quite achieved enough to feel happy or satisfied.

You've worked hard and tried to be a good person, but had some genuine bad luck and got shafted by people you trusted. All your wife did when you met her was giggle, suck, and fuck, until she had a ring on her finger, two kids, a house, and an SUV, and then turned into some kind of Darth Vader/Nora Batty hybrid, kicked your arse out and denied you access to your kids.

To these men, a life in which you got the breaks, the

house, the clothes, the lifestyle, the money, and screwed birds till your penis fainted gets a double thumbs up, irrespective of the consequences. Be remembered as a monster? No problem. Your family name disgraced? So be it. Your estate and business closed down, pensioners left in poverty? Good, let'em fucking starve.

Unless you take the "eventually" out again. Not eventually...now! Horrible things should happen to horrible people early in life, when it hurts, when they've got plenty of time to stew, lament and regret. Somebody get the bastard before he does something else! We need a time limit.

How about, "What goes around comes around within two to three years." That'll make people think twice. They'll get their comeuppance early doors and everybody's happy. You don't have to kill them; humiliation is better.

A lot of catchphrases and sayings we hold to be true are not. "The early bird catches the worm." In other words, the worm that stays in bed lives to tell the story. This is just encouraging laziness.

You don't see worms anymore do you? When you were kids, you'd beat the grass with your hands to make the worms think it was raining. They'd come up out the ground and you'd mash them, cutting them in half to see if both ends would wiggle away.

The worms caught on to this little caper, and stopped coming to the surface. That's why you don't see them anymore. They've all drowned. Well, again, now we have to pay the price. Soil erosion and the emergence of flooding are mainly due to the lack of worms. When it was wet and earth was washing away, the worms used to drink the water. They would then link their bodies together and squeeze, holding the soil together in a bid to stop their homes washing away. Not only are there less worms, the ones left are half the size, meaning they're less effective for giving the soil a bit of body and hold-togetherness.

"He who laughs last, laughs longest." In reality, he who laughs last didn't get the joke, and is laughing to hide his embarrassment at his piss-poor joke getting. I told my friends this one day, ensuring they all now scramble to laugh at even my most casual observations, none wanting to be last. One of my pals will only go to the toilet when I do, in case I tell a funny whilst he's in there and can't get out in time to avoid being the final laugh.

"Never eat yellow snow." Quite frankly, if you've reached the stage where you're living off snow you could do with some variety in your diet. What if the yellow bits are custard?

"People who live in glass houses shouldn't throw stones." Well people who live in brick houses shouldn't throw stones either; they'll have somebody's eye out. People who live in glass houses tend to throw stones during the summer, when living in a glass house can be very hot and stuffy, making it hard for them to sleep at night and pretty cranky as a result. People who live in glass houses should avoid installing gravel drives (and therefore temptation), and maybe invest in an air cooler.

Okay. Let's lighten things up a little. I can see some of your eyes are glazing over, so let's take a little break. How about some jokes?

A rabbit goes into a pub:

RABBIT: Pint of lager please.

BARMAN: Sorry, we don't serve rabbits – your teeth chip the glasses.

An elephant walks into an illegal bookmaker's:

BOOKMAKER: For fuck's sake! Can't you see we're trying to keep a low profile here, you big-eared twat!

Or a limerick:

There once was a footballer from Dundee
Who had an extremely sore knee
He went to the physio
Who gave him some ultrasound
After that he was fine.

There once was a man from Sri Lanka
Who tired of being called a wanker
He said why would I
Risk getting spunk in my eye
For the sake of two minutes on the hand pump.

An Englishman, Irishman, and Scotsman walk into a pub. The Englishman says something deeply, deeply offensive to every ethnic group in the room, the Scotsman refuses to buy a drink and the Irishman blows the place up.

Ah, the joy of stereotypes. Some of you are now probably thinking, enough of the jokes, hilarious as they are, let's get back to the important stuff. I would say that jokes are very important, as are comedians, and stereotypes are useful in formulating policies that actually work.

Imagine the next big world crisis. People are dying, genocide, threats of war being exchanged. Do you send in the bureaucrats and envoys? No. You send in a comedian. Instantly, the atmosphere changes. It's hard to take someone seriously when a comedian's just implied they might be gay because of their shirt.

Send Bill Bailey and a piano into Northern Ireland and the troubles will soon be long forgotten. Send Reeves & Mortimer into Palestine and they'll be too confused to fight. Dispatch Michael McIntyre to Kashmir and everybody will be skipping by teatime, whilst Victoria Wood would have Iranian women singing songs about getting spanked with a Woman's Weekly.

This approach has its limits. I wouldn't have sent Bernard Manning to Zimbabwe, and if you let Roy Chubby Brown anywhere near North Korea you better have a fall-out shelter in your garden.

How are stereotypes positive? I'll tell you. I saw a Scouser the other day, and there he was...big shaggy haircut, a moustache and a shell suit. I couldn't believe it, a real life stereotype.

If you saw one in the street you'd run up to him, and start shouting, "Calm down! Calm down!" and laugh heartily. Many people see these characters as an unfortunate reminder of Liverpool's imperialist past, when Scouse hordes roamed Europe raiding Sergio Tacchini and Lacoste stores to pay for their trips to the footy.

But Liverpool should embrace these figures; they're Liverpool's answer to Beefeaters. A throw back to a distant time when Frankie Goes To Hollywood ruled the charts,

Liverpool won the league every year, and people tuned-in in their millions to watch Brookside. Get them to guard important buildings in full uniform. Bright shiny shell suits, perms, trainers, holding long bits of four-by-two. Embrace your history.

A world run by stereotypes would be much safer than the present day version, in which unpredictability and diversity make long term planning so difficult.

Let's try a Scottish stereotype. The Scottish hate the English, but love heroin. So introduce National Service. Five months in boot camp will get them off the smack, then march on London.

The Welsh stereotype involves choirs, rugby, and banging sheep. Solution? Abolish school. The Welsh can spend their mornings singing, and their afternoons playing rugby. With the pitiful margins in sheep farming it'll be more profitable to turn sheep farms into full blown brothels, meaning after a hard day singing and scrummaging they can spend their evenings "unwinding." Singing, shagging, and rugby; what's not to like?

Like most lads brought up in rural areas I remember having a go at "lamb-pumping," as we used to call it. I actually enjoyed sheep-shagging but gave it up through insecurity. It's impossible to tell when a sheep has an orgasm, and I began to worry I wasn't satisfying them. As I wandered past fields I became paranoid if they all started baaing when they saw me. One day I was convinced I heard one of them saying I was hung like a lamb. I started masturbating before I had sex with the sheep so I could last longer and put on a better show, and holding a mirror in front of them to see if their facial expressions changed at any point. In the end I stopped my woolly-bullying and refused to go near a farm until all my farmyard conquests were long since slaughtered and eaten.

One in three people from Essex will rob a bank at some point in their lives. This is why many young women from Essex join the army and go to fight in Afghanistan and Iraq, because it's safer than staying at home and getting a job at Barclays in Braintree.

Essex lads who get caught blagging should be seconded to the Treasury, where they can get false IDs and passports and then dispatched into Europe to rob banks and depositories. The Italian Job proved you can't beat a good continental blag. If the Eastern Europeans want to flood over in their millions to make loads of money and take it home, the least we can do is dispatch some naughty geezers to rob some of it back. Why spend thousands housing these boys in prison when you can turn them into a profit centre?

All Irish people are religious bigots and terrorists who spend the whole time fighting over whether they're British or Irish. The solution? Abolish Catholicism and Protestantism, and convert Northern Ireland to Buddhism. Not only will everybody be the same religion, two hours of meditation a day might calm everyone down a bit. You then physically detach Northern Ireland from Ireland, tow it north and declare it an independent Scandinavian state.

Everybody in Manchester loves music, football and dancing, but is fed up with gang, knife and gun culture so bad the police now call the city "Gunchester." Listen up. Everybody found in possession of a knife or a gun is to be shot in both hands, both feet and kneecapped. Not being able to play an instrument, dance, or play football is ten times worse than killing a Manc. If you catch one drink-driving, don't ban them from driving, ban them from putting gravy on their chips, it'll drive them "fookin'mad."

If a lad from Salford is being anti-social, don't give them a standard ASBO, i.e. one that prevents him coming within one hundred yards of his patch. Give him a turbo ASBO, i.e. one that prevents him from going within a hundred yards of Old Trafford. He'll do whatever you want. Communicate with people in the language their stereotype understands.

Geordies are double hard bastards, who don't feel the cold, drink beer and, you guessed it, love their football. Cut electricity to Newcastle. Energy wastage is a massive problem in this country, and if the Geordies don't feel the cold they don't need central heating. Most of the televisions and lighting still run on oil in Newcastle so it's not as if much will change, apart from one thing. With no electricity, Newcastle United will have nothing to power the floodlights or heat the pitch during winter.

Set the Geordies targets concerning crime, vandalism and anti-social behaviour. If these targets are being met, electricity will be restored to Newcastle for home matches. If not, they forfeit the points.

How about country folk? Country bumpkins like hunting and cider, and hate outsiders, townies, and ethnic minorities. Convert every barn in England into a mosque. When the cockerel is now woken every morning by the call to prayers he can find out what it feels like. As I've already suggested, criminals can be used as legitimate prey for hunting, and a Government programme to plant thirty million cider trees will see cheap cider for all and an end to global warming. Every country tavern must be required by law to have rooms upstairs to bang the wenches for a farthing.

Are you all still with me? Sit up and stop slouching. Are you chewing?

You probably noticed a consistent football theme running through that last bit. Sport in general is the answer to many of our problems, and it's not just about being good enough to be a professional athlete.

During the nineteenth century, the working classes were told to avoid exercise. Fitness was an invention of the bourgeoisie, designed to drain any energy the working classes still had when they got home from work, meaning they were too puffed out for revolution. Nowadays attitudes have changed.

The answer to boredom? Grass-roots sport. The answer to gang culture? Grass-roots sport. The answer to petty crime? Grass-roots sport. The answer to the breakdown in community spirit? Grass-roots sport.

We're locked in an epidemic of high blood pressure, diabetes, high cholesterol, record levels of stress and depression, and kids who can't focus or concentrate. The answer? Gr...you know what.

Cut funding to the terminally ill. Let them die and build some sports facilities instead. Flatten all flowerbeds and turn them into football pitches. Gardens do nothing but harm and waste valuable grass. If there's one group the Eco-Nazis should be targeting, it's gardeners. The reason we get water shortages is because the flowers are drinking all the bloody water.

Flowers are firing out the pollen that makes many

people's lives unbearable during the summer. Every year people's hay fever gets worse, their noses more runny, and their sneezes bigger. People will soon be sneezing so hard their head comes off, leaving huge geezers of snot erupting from their severed necks.

The next time a wasp stings you and you're trying to find the culprit? He's in the flowers. They're hiding him. Refuse them water until they send the wasp out.

Anyway. In order to help England's chances on the sporting stage I recently approached Lucozade with a helpful suggestion. Isotonic lager. The alcohol will kill you eventually but in the meantime we'd all be as fit as fiddles; fit enough to run off the beer belly. England, Ireland, Scotland and Wales will dominate every sport in the world, closely followed by Australia, New Zealand and South Africa.

We'd all be dead before we reach forty, but as I've already told you, an ageing population is no good to anybody, and there's nothing worse than an old has-been banging on about how great they were or how rubbish and overpaid today's stars are.

But if the British are to attain sporting supremacy more is needed than isotonic beer and better sporting facilities. We need to inspire the grass-roots with sterling performances. For a start, we need to abandon all the new fangled sports psychology bullshit and get back to basics.

Take cricket. For years, the English couldn't beat the Australians at cricket, and decided that new modern psychology was needed. During a match the average Englishman stood out on the boundary going through his self-actualisation programmes, thinking positive, and concentrating on maintaining positive body language. Every now and again he yelled something daft in the belief it helped with team spirit. When it was time for him to bowl he was confused, tired, his hands were numb from too much clapping and he struggled with his appeals because he'd lost his voice.

The average Australian bowler stood on the boundary without a care in the world. For him, positive body language was taking a regular sip from the tinny he'd hidden in his pants. Quietly singing the dirty version of Waltzing Matilda, he placed one hand down the front of his pants, the other one up his nose. When he got bored, he switched hands. When it was his turn to bowl, he was relaxed. His hands were warm and moist, his fingertips were sticky, and his throat was lubricated. He was ready to go.

England did briefly become the best team in the world, a feat we achieved by picking as many South Africans as possible. All this hides the fact that English sportsmen are still too soft.

In Australia, kids have it much tougher than in England. When kids are born in Australia they don't hang mobiles over the cot, they hang killer bats for the kids to wrestle with. When they're teething, they are given scorpions to chew on. That's how they get the Australian accent.

In Australia, you have to check your footwear in case there's a scorpion in there. In Britain the nastiest surprise kids endure in the mornings is finding your big brother has wanked in your slippers. Unless you're a Catholic, in which case waking up next to Father O'Hagan in his milkmaid costume is always a downer.

Every time the English play a former colony they raise their game to avenge the injustices of the past. If an Englishman once trod on your uncle's bunion it's all the motivation you need to score a century. There aren't many countries the British haven't invaded or upset, and the Welsh, Scottish, and Irish in turn hate the English even more than all the others added together.

The English have also been invaded of course, but choose to embrace their history, i.e. celebrate "what the Romans done for us." This lack of bitterness has made the English soft. It's time for us to stop celebrating our history and start resenting it. When we play the Italians at football or rugby, flatten Pierluigi and tell him, "That's for Boudicea!" When we play the Scandinavians at football, boot Torsten up the arse and growl, "That's for raping and pillaging my great, great, great, great, great, great, great, great, great, great, great, grandmother!.......You cunt."

The French must be made to pay for 1066, Napoleon and Orangina, the Portuguese bashed up for Magellan, and the Austrians attacked for the scheming of Metternich. When the American tennis players turn up for Wimbledon, chuck all their stuff into the harbour to see how they like it.

Revenge must be taken on Scotland for the Krankies, the Proclaimers, the invasion of Wembley in 1977, Wet Wet Wet, and George Galloway. The Irish must be held to account for Bono's incessant whining about Africa, Kilkenny beer, and Graham Norton.

The Irish have for years used the British to hide their own shortcomings. Everything is the fault of the evil imperialist British, and yet surely, slowly, bit-by-bit, the Irish have been invading the globe in the form of pubs.

There is now an Irish pub in every town, village, and city on the globe. There are more Irish pubs in Britain now than post offices. There are more Irish pubs on this planet than soldiers. When Lord Lucan is finally discovered it will be in an Irish pub in a village in the Costa Rican rainforest. When Mark Thatcher was lost in the desert the only thing that saved him was coming across an O'Neill's Irish pub, where he got a fry-up and five pints of Guinness before moving on.

When a man whose name I forget stepped out of the tent and said, "I may be gone some time," it was because he'd spotted O'Flannigan's Fun Pub two hundred yards away and fancied a good drink. When the human race finally does land some probes on Neptune, the first thing they'll see is a blackboard with "LIVE SKY FOOTBALL SHOWN HERE," on a blackboard outside O'Reilly's Sports Bar.

When the Irish invade the world it will be with an army of publicans and bar staff. It'll be remembered as the greatest trick played by an invading force since the great horse of Troy. The population of Ireland is little more than four million, but the huge amount of Irish people now spread across Britain, Australia, the USA, Canada and the rest of the globe masks the fact there are now six hundred and fifty million Irish people living on this planet, exercising a concept the Nazis called "Lebensraum."

Being Catholic and opposed to contraception, the Irish have now expanded and multiplied beyond control, a bit like the Agent Smith program in the Matrix movies. The main reason Bono is so concerned about Africa is that by the year 2053, 25% of the population of Africa will be Irish, and a starving population means empty pubs, and nobody to muck out the stables and work the stalls at the races.

Bill Gates is apparently calling off his attempts to woo the Indians and the Chinese in the realisation that the Irish will soon wield more global clout than the US and Russia combined. The next version of Windows is rumoured to be in Gaelic, and programmed to crash for four days every year whilst the Cheltenham Festival is on. The UN are also rumoured to be changing their motto from "We The Peoples" to "Here's m'hand, here's m'heart young fella" to reflect this global power shift.

The Irish now have a huge, highly motivated expeditionary force, all established in their own bases with a good supply of food and beer, and half the enemy are pissed up in the bar.

At a prearranged signal, every Irish pub in Tenerife, Magaluf, Lanzarote, Ibiza, the Algarve and Benidorm will place signs outside their bars advertising pints of vodka and orange for 30p, with re-runs of Only Fools and Horses to be shown on a twenty-four hour loop.

Within five hours, 80% of Englishmen under the age of twenty-one will be doubled up from laughing, and pissed as parrots. England will be defenceless, and the invasion will begin. First they'll take New York, and North London, followed by Luton, Boston, and Reading.

We need to prepare ourselves for the worst. The English will be forced to live off a diet of mouldy potatoes to see how we like it, and all the Church of England Christians will be made to live in areas segregated from the Catholics. Every year during marching season, thousands of Irish will march through Church of England neighbourhoods to celebrate

Johnny Logan's defeat of the British at the Eurovision Song Contest of 1987.

Angel Cake makers will be forced to change the layers in the cake to orange, green and white, whilst English youngsters with Irish parents or grandparents will be known as "muggles" or "mudbloods" and have to endure bullying from the "pure-paddies."

Go to your homes and prepare. The Irish are coming and they're not the only ones.

The population of India is set to increase by 500 million over the next 50 years. If half of those are men, that's quarter of a million potential fast bowlers, spin bowlers and batsmen all dying for the chance to stuff the English cricket team out of sight. We've got enough on our plate trying to beat Australia, a country with a population half the size of ours.

Of course the reason we lose at football is our hair is too short and we're pants at taking penalties. Years ago English footballers would have stepped up to take a penalty believing God was on England's side and scoring was the natural order. Nowadays, scoring that penalty is tantamount to invading that poor foreigners country and distinctly racist. So they miss.

Put Spectre in charge of the England team. The wife or girlfriend of any English footballer who misses a penalty during a shoot-out should be murdered. Any England player who hates his missus may take the opportunity to deliberately miss (have some of that, you bitch) but this is less likely than the propensity of the modern Englishman to blaze one into the stand and start booing like an Italian whose mama's just died, seconds after treading on a tear gas canister.

The countries that win the World Cup on a regular basis are the ones with the long hair. Argentina, Brazil, and Italy's players all have Alice-bands, headbands, and ponytails; tearing down the wing with their hair blowing in the wind. Okay, not the Germans, but I refuse to accept they've ever won the World Cup.

This is the problem. The English, as well as the Welsh, Scottish, and Irish are all mad mental skinheads or pretty boys with coiffures from Toni & Guy. What we need are pretty players with long hair, but devious and sly. Vicious, conniving sods with no personality, but angelic looks and lots of flowing locks; a cross between Simon Cowell and Kelly Brook. Every single English black player should have the haircut and morals of Don King but the cheeky grin of Bill Cosby.

Long hair makes you stronger. Samson proved that a man loses all his strength and va-va-voom when his hair is cut. I myself can feel quite lethargic when I get my back waxed. All the top Premiership clubs have squads of nutritionists, psychologists, and fitness coaches to advise their players on how to look after themselves, when the Latins have proved all you need is long hair and loads of red wine and shagging.

During the days of Samson, people were thrown to the lions, or forced to fight for their freedom against gladiators. Chariot racing was a brutal, often fatal pastime. I can't think of one person who has died recently in the British sporting arena. We are being cheated.

We need the return of the coliseums; watching people being ripped to pieces by lions followed by chariot races around the bullring in Birmingham. We can do a fly on the wall documentary in the hospitals treating the casualties (a bit like Animal Hospital but NOT hosted by Rolf Harris), and all cry when a gladiator gets put down.

Nothing burns calories like danger. In such a world, we wouldn't have to worry so obsessively about diet. When I was a kid we lived off chips, fizzy drinks, custard, and crisps, but we weren't fat because we had active lifestyles. We went scrumping, nicked stuff from the farmer, shoplifted and vandalised things. We'd smash bottles and eat dog poo, which in those days stayed on the pavement so long in summer it went white and was frequently mistaken for nougat.

Despite our behaviour, we had an inherent respect for authority and consequences of getting caught, i.e. a fucking good leathering from the old man, the cane from the headmaster, or running home with a dog hanging off your arse.

Nowadays kids just pull a knife or a gun and it's the grown-ups that are running, with some vegan Communist running alongside them reminding them how it's their fault. However, running away stopped me getting fat. The thrill of a good chase burnt double the calories I could eat in an evening. Kids don't run away nowadays, and that's why they'll have diabetes and heart attacks before their GCSEs. And do you know what? Good. The next decade will see the phenomenon of people laughing at kids' funerals, throwing chips instead of roses down on the coffin and saying, "That'll teach you to stand your ground you fat little prick!"

The Mayor of London, by the way, has unearthed a scheme for addressing the unhealthy eating habits of Londoners. It's called the Indigestion Charge.

Anybody intending to enter a fast food joint, curry house

or kebab shop in central London must pay the Indigestion Charge. No shop will be allowed to serve you unless you have a receipt to prove you paid the charge, or proof you live in the area.

All day we're bombarded with people screaming at us to eat more fwesh fwoot and veggy-ter-bulls. We're now meant to ditch the junk food and convert to a new health regime. Surely getting people to eat a mixture is best – half junk, half healthy. A Big Mac and two apples, a bacon sarnie and two bananas, or a salad followed by a big bit of cake. You get the comfort of the calories from the naughty stuff and the benefit of the healthy stuff. I call it a fifty / fifty diet.

Use chocolate as a reward. You run two miles, you get a bar of chocolate. Hardcore chocoholics are going to get their hands on some chocolate one way or another, at least this way they get some exercise as well. Kids would happily eat a bowl of bran flakes if there were a Lion Bar at the end of it, and if they're exercising they can burn off the calories.

Gun and knife amnesties? A free bar of chocolate with every weapon handed in. Chocolate for doing homework. Chocolate for cleaning your room. Give a panda some chocolate and he'll be bonking all night.

Don't under-estimate the persuasive qualities of chocolate. When I was a kid at school, the caretaker told us that Milky Bars were made with the spunk of Willy Wonka, and we believed him, but we still ate them anyway. The caretaker, who as you remember, had Anal Dairy Disorder, also used to tell us that if we stuck the Milky Bar up our bums we'd get pregnant and give birth to an Oompa Loompa. He offered to prove it, but even I didn't fall for that one.

Chocolate must be given on the NHS to people with mild depression, or people who've lost their job. Income Support should include a ration of chocolate. Potholers never set off without a couple of Aeros in their bag, and it's not just for the energy. When a friend of mine found himself trapped in a flooding cave, he survived by sucking an Aero bar and breathing the oxygen in the bubbles.

Being so absorbent, Crunchies make excellent flood defences. That's why Cadbury's factories never flood. If you have athlete's foot, crumble a Flake and rub it between your toes. Curly-Wurlys have been used to mend tennis nets during professional tennis matches and separated Kinder Eggs have been used by vets to nurture abandoned chicklings.

A world dominated by chocolate works on so many levels. With the war on drugs being won, the Columbians will start to switch their cocoa fields away from cocaine into safe, profitable chocolate production.

Kids on a fifty/fifty diet will now be getting a potent blend of vitamins and energy. The teacher will have to tell them off for studying too hard and neglecting their mates. They'll be running around the football field like the England manager was watching, and too high on choco-adrenaline to be nasty.

Women can have chocolate on the NHS. The menopause, period pains, migraines, obsessing over shoes; all these female conditions will disappear overnight.

There is more we can do to help the weighbridge worriers. All fat people must be placed on small islands until they are a reasonable size. This is not just about social exclusion and stigmatising lardies; there is a sound scientific theory behind this idea, and the answer lies with elephants.

Why are there no elephants in Britain? There were a few at some point; the Romans brought them. Thousands of years before, Britain was attached to the rest of Europe, and elephants wandered freely across Britain on route to somewhere else. But since Britain became an island, elephants have never been part of the indigenous population. Let me explain why.

Britain is too small. Big creatures don't flourish in small countries. They need room to roam and explore. An elephant decides to roll around on the floor; he rolls too far in one direction, falls off the island and into the sea. He decides to have a wash in the river, slips, falls over, and a tidal wave hits Oxford. If elephants had evolved in Britain, they would be much smaller, comparable in size to a cow, or possibly a large pony.

That's why there are no rhinoceroses in Wales. You don't see any whales in canals, or hippos in Winchester. Tropical fish grow to a size that fits the tank you put them in. Creatures adapt to the size of their surroundings.

All fat people must be deported to the Isle of Wight, with Royal Navy cruisers around the edge to stop anyone leaving. If anyone does try and swim for it, allow them to swim to Britain (or drown in the attempt) and then pick them up and take them back to the island – "Good! Now do it again!"

In time the sludge-guts will shrink to fit their surroundings, preferably before the island sinks or succumbs to heavy flooding.

The Navy, by the way, has a traditional nautical method for dealing with obesity whilst at sea. All the crew get a plimsoll line painted on their belly. When the fattingtons complain about being hungry they fling them overboard. If they sink past the line they are already overloaded, and denied any more food.

Place treadmills and rowing machines in people's houses, and wire them up to electricity generators. People will then get a limited amount of electricity. If they want any more they need to work for it.

I read a newspaper article in which an academic advocated rationing the amount of electricity people get, in order to force them to use it more sparingly.

Apparently they tried this in Russia, but only succeeded in creating the Russian Mafia. When the Russian authorities began to ration electricity in the late fifties, a huge thriving black market in bootleg electricity began. Huge underground sweatshops made their own electricity, powered by thousands of rats, mice, hamsters, guinea pigs and Siberians running on treadmills attached to dynamos.

For a while the Politburo tolerated their activities, until the infamous Brinx-Mattski electricity robbery, when the Mafia broke into the Leningrad power station and stole enough electricity to keep the city going for a year.

This could have been avoided if they'd let the fatties get fit whilst generating some extra "lekky." With the amount of subcutaneous fat they carry it's not as if salad dodgers feel the cold too much, so they won't need to generate much for heating. As they start losing weight they'll need more but as they get fitter they'll be able to row / run more.

As everybody knows, the main reason given for obesity in our children is that they spend too much time sat indoors playing computer games, rather than outside running around, playing and exercising. Make the kids exercise to generate the electricity to play their computer game. As the gamers lose weight they'll become fitter, sharper and mentally more alert, helping to generate a record score or even finish the game. Once these kids get fit and lose weight it'll give them the confidence to take up a proper sport.

As usual, there is a catch. Sport is a wonderful tool for social progress, but beware of people trying to exploit it. Despite what I've just said, sport is not the answer to everything, and in some cases, is downright inappropriate. I'll give you an example.

Every now and again, something comes along so ridiculous that you almost lose control of your bodily functions. Something that makes your jaw drop so hard that it bounces back and snaps your teeth together like a crocodile.

Such a moment recently arrived for me when I read about the football World Cup for the Homeless. I'll say that again; the Homeless fucking World fucking Cup. All the homeless people of the world coming together to compete in a global football tournament. It's difficult to know where to start.

For a start, homelessness is something we're meant to be fighting. Something bad that we're committed to abolishing, not nurturing by making homelessness a route to the fame and glory of a World Cup winner's medal.

We live in a world where winning Division Seven East of the Scunthorpe & District Sunday League is more important to some men than their own children. If their kids were murdered on a Sunday morning, these blokes would step over their bodies to get their kitbag and go to football, and if they came straight home afterwards it would only be because they lost.

Premier League referees now receive death threats for making bad decisions, whilst most Premiership football managers would happily stamp on their grandmother's throat to win a football match. In such a world, making it possible to win a Homeless World Cup is only encouraging more people to live rough.

The Homeless World Cup. What's next? Wimbledon for victims of domestic abuse? The Boat Race for people that tried and failed to commit suicide? How about the Open Golf Championship for people with schizophrenia (they'll have to fill-out two cards and play four-balls with only two players.)

Let's have a World Snooker Championship for people with CCJs against their name. How about a London Marathon for agoraphobics or maybe a Twickenham Sevens rugby tournament for people that self-harm. That could get really messy.

If homeless people have enough energy and dedication to compete in an international football tournament they've got enough to get a job and somewhere to live. What's the point in winning a trophy when you've got no mantelpiece to put it on?

What are the Brits' chances of dominating homeless football in the long run? Virtually none. There may be too many homeless people in Britain but we're nothing compared to the rest of the world. Do shanty-towns count as being homeless? A piece of corrugated iron is no more use than a cardboard box if you think about it.

With a much smaller pool of players, England are bound

to struggle. Not only that, the countries with the largest homeless populations will now claim their policy of ignoring the homeless is the reason they are now a major football power. Maybe we should make it easier to repossess people's homes in this country and do less to help the homeless so we can develop a larger playing pool and dominate the world of homeless footy.

How long do you have to be homeless to qualify for the tournament? My contacts on the street tell me David Beckham is so desperate to win a World Cup he's decided to live rough until he qualifies. The only hitch is image rights. Under the terms of his agreement with the tournament organisers, every homeless person on the planet would be due an image rights payment to Beckham, threatening to land FNASFA (Federation of Non-Abode Specific Football Associations) with a bill for US$350m.

If the homeless can have their own sports events why not their own government? A homeless prime minister, living in a big posh cardboard box on Kensington High Street with a police constable stood guard outside.

Some of you may think I have a problem with homeless people, even a lack of empathy and understanding with their plight. This is not true. In fact, I think a government for homeless people would be a great way to deliver key services where it's needed most, and there is a precedent.

In the mid-eighties, the Socialist government in France introduced politicians for the homeless. It was the government's hair-brained response to accusations they had lost touch with the problems of the least fortunate.

The elections were fraught with difficulty. The homeless right wing were accused of gerrymandering after being caught sneaking their cardboard boxes into key areas the night before polling, and the left were exposed giving their friends preferential treatment on council cardboard boxes by the coast.

The Minister for Housing became confused as to the purpose of his role. Was he trying to get all homeless people housed? Or provide better accommodation for the homeless, even though this would make them less keen to re-join the world of accommodation?

The Foreign Minister spent most of his time in Jamaica on fact-finding missions, eventually returning with eleven thousand hammocks for the homeless to sleep on. Chaos ensued; the avenues and boulevards of gay Paree cut off by homeless people stringing their hammocks from one side to the other.

Every time a homeless politician rose to the top and showed potential he was offered a job by Lord Sugar and resigned. In addition to this, corruption was rife. The Homeless Secretary had to resign after the "Special Brew for Questions" enquiry, which found MHPs were agreeing to ask certain questions in the Caravan of Commons in return for super-strength lager.

Like everything else in France, the whole venture ended in tears, strikes and demonstrations, and the homeless wandered back into the wilderness. I would suggest a more simplified pragmatic approach to the problem.

I propose the reforestation of Britain. Huge rambling forests of oaks and pines and stuff and such. With designated treehouse areas where rural flower-power hippy homeless people can live in the trees like Kevin Costner's mob in Robin Hood. Only in designated areas though;

there must be parts where the public can go and ramble and enjoy nature without being mugged for their socks and roll-ups.

What about the urban homeless? Those who like to stay close to the city and off-licences. How about dog kennels? There are at the moment thousands of dog kennels sat in large compounds around the country, unused and unneeded by the dog community. When was the last time you went to somebody's house and saw a kennel?

Dogs now get to sleep inside in the warm. Some people even let them sleep in the bed with them. If you allocated these kennels to homeless people it would give them a base. A roof over their head and something to keep the wind out. A space of their own. Put a large padded basket in it, some blankets and pillows and a dog's life has never seemed so good. It's no different to camping.

On a similar theme, the long-term unemployed must be housed in sheds. It's not right they should have houses when people who are working hard can't afford a place of their own to live.

Housing people in kennels and sheds is a good idea, but it won't happen, for two reasons. Firstly, too many people will see it as disrespectful. In our PR, spin-obsessed, on-message culture putting people in kennels would be implying they are no better than dogs, and putting people in a shed puts them on a par with a jar of screws or a garden strimmer. No it doesn't. They are just wooden houses. That's all. Who cares how big they are or what they get used for normally? They'll do the job.

The second reason is the British obsession with bricks and mortar. Houses are cheaper in America because they build them out of wood. If you want cheap affordable housing, log cabins are the way forward. I'd love to live in a log cabin. Who wouldn't? Center Parcs is the way forward, the housing estate of the future.

Housing is an emotive issue. When the economy struggles, the first thing everybody focuses on is the housing market. When people get a pay rise, they immediately look at an extension to their house, or a new kitchen or bathroom. Having a home you can call your own is the most important thing a family can have. For some, a big house is the ultimate status symbol.

And what about third world housing? Everyone bangs on about the need to preserve the rainforests, but nobody thinks about the indigenous rain forest population. These people have no houses, no basic services or police force. The rainforest has six hundred and six percent humidity in summer and yet many Amazonians are left without so much as a radiator to dry their socks on.

Do you think the Amazonians would want to live in their wonderful indigenous environments if the alternative was a council house in Swindon, with flushing toilet, Sky television, a good curry house on the corner and a decent speedway team? I don't think so.

You really want to solve the problems of the third world? Give them what they really need. Anyone in the British ethnic minority community will tell you the main reason people are so hacked off in the third world is not famine or war, but the lack of proper pubs and quality beer.

When someone does open a pub very few people can afford to drink in it. Cheap affordable beer is a far more pressing concern for these people than housing or global warming. The hotter the planet gets, the more pressing the need for cold lager. Beer might not solve all of life's problems but it sure feels like it sometimes, and that's a start.

When the royalties begin to flow from my writing I intend to launch Beer-Aid, and get celebrities and hard-drinking sports stars to tour areas of the world where people are forced to contemplate a life in which they'll never get pissed, and be sober every time they eat curry.

During Beer-Aid, in between documentary films, we can have drinking games in the studio, and get well-known news presenters to drink a yard of ale and puke for the viewing public. All the puke will be stored in a gunk tank, and deposited on the head of a famous macro-biotic, vegetarian, yoga practising, sober fuck-wit actor who thinks we give a flying fuck about Tibet. (The Chinese produce the cheapest washing machines so let's keep them sweet.)

Peanuts and crisps will also be airlifted to the third world to help the new beer drinkers soak up their ale and make them thirstier in the process. Of course the people of Africa don't ideally want charity and free beer and crisps. What they want is the chance to work their way out of sobriety by brewing their own beer and growing their own crops to make Scampi Fries and Monster Munch.

If we can successfully divert the sea through Africa, just spray the salt water straight onto the potato fields, producing the world's first genuine ready salted crisps.

Beer-Aid will open local breweries and build wells to supply water for beer. In some third world countries women have to walk ten miles per day to fetch water for ropey home brew, frequently being killed by elephants pissed up on bootleg Bacardi Breezer.

Surely the hot weather in Africa is tailor-made for growing grapes with which to make red wine? All we need is some chalk for the soil and you're laughing.

Third world sobriety has to stop. Every thirty seconds, somebody in Africa thinks, "I could fucking murder a pint." Together we can sort this mess out once and for all. Say no to beerlessness.

It's no good just blaming everything on the government and politicians, but most people do. Politicians inevitably take it in the neck from celebrities with causes, because in a perfect world the politicians wouldn't let these situations develop in the first place.

Surely the answer is to put celebs and pop stars in charge of the government and all the world's problems will disappear double lively. Except they won't because then the famous and pretty will come up against all the stuff that politicians come up against and it will dawn on them that maybe life isn't as easy as they thought, have a nervous breakdown and book themselves into the Priory after precisely twenty-three seconds.

So get off the politician's backs; be grateful they're prepared to take on a job you couldn't cope with for less money a year than a footballer earns in a weekend. So what if their expenses claims are a bit on the fruity side? They're cheap at a tenth of the price.

The problem is not politicians but the electorate. Earlier I outlined the great things that stupid people do, but that doesn't mean you should let them vote. It's quite simple; you must pass a basic political general knowledge test to get your vote. Why should people have to pass a test? Let me explain.

You take your car to be fixed. Before the mechanic starts, you take five minutes to ask him or her some basic questions (let's say he's a man for simplicity.) You find that he knows absolutely nothing about cars. He thinks the steering wheel is a ride at the fairground, the clutch is Starsky's best mate, and a carburettor is the creamy spaghetti his girlfriend cooked him Friday night.

That is not all. He's actually proud of the fact he knows nothing about your car. He boasts about the fact he hates cars and the motor trade because, "They're all in it for themselves."

Would you trust this bloke to fix your motor? No. Would you let a man who hated biology and despised people become a surgeon? Would you let an atheist become a priest? Would you let somebody who couldn't count do your accounts?

And yet we let people who, "Hates dem politicians and takes no interest cos day-iz all in it for themselves, innit," vote. Madness. Think about it. Your country is in the hands of politicians who won with the votes of people with no knowledge of, or interest in, what they were doing. Is this a good thing? (No.)

Politicians constantly witter on about the need to communicate better, but always fail in their attempts. Instead of trying to find ever more clever ways to communicate, they need to dumb it down:

"Public sector pay restraint is important, because the less money we give the workers, the less they have to spend on drugs and cigarettes."

"Men are to be sterilised after the age of thirty, to cut

down on the amount of kids they produce in their lifetime. In addition, every woman who has nine children will have each subsequent child confiscated or her box filled with Polyfilla."

You can't bring seven kids up properly. I'm convinced you can't. Surely each kid demands a certain amount of attention in order to look after it properly and there is only so much time in the day. If you have too many kids they will all become compulsive attention seekers from spending their whole childhood competing for their parents' time.

It's no good trying to reason with these people, and you can't ask them to stop shagging. For the ones who smoke and don't exercise sex is the only time they get to take a deep, clean breath; they'd suffocate.

Any woman with four kids before her twentieth birthday should have her fanny shaved and featured on Crimewatch. "Has anyone seen this fanny? It's responsible for producing four of the most stupid violent kids ever seen in Sunderland. If you see the fanny, do not approach, as a fifth potential criminal is rumoured to be due out of it any day now."

When women like this are giving birth, the police should be present to taser the baby as it comes out. It'll kick start its breathing better than a slap on the arse and stop the little sod stealing anything whilst you tag it.

As usual, the real blame lies with men. Eleven kids by seven different women? Tie a knot in it you Neanderthal spunk cannon. At least women are limited somewhat, in that they can only have one kid every nine months (okay, they might have twins or triplets, but you get my drift.) Men can have as many kids in a nine-month period as women they can screw in that time. Get five women pregnant in one day, and nine months later five kids will normally be the result.

Of course, if you confront their behaviour, they miraculously become Catholic. Never been to Church, never prayed, broke every commandment in the book. A life of unholy sin from the moment they got their first erection, but mention contraception and they're proclaiming their loyalty to the Pope, opposition to condoms and crossing themselves like an Argentinian footballer.

One of my mates off the estate had three kids by the age of nineteen. His dad sneaked into his bedroom whilst he was sleeping off a session in the pub and injected his gonads with quick drying cement. He never conceived another child and his girlfriend came to love the sensation of his plums banging against her like mini-wrecking balls during sex.

This is where the Big Sister™ inner thigh laser pads security system could come into play. Force women to wear it at night. When the lasers get broken, an alarm goes off in the police station, and the police come round and shoot the woman with a tranquilliser dart filled with a liquid version of the morning-after pill. Alternatively, every ten years, every kid under the age of two must be killed. Maybe Herod's role in history should be re-vamped a wee bit, as the original "over-crowding tsar."

Overcrowding and population explosion is not just a human problem. Animals are not helping, and need to be controlled more effectively. Elephants, bison and gazelles roam the continent kicking up a right old stink. In addition to the noise generated, they trample over what wildlife there is to be found, wading through the rivers and disturbing the fragile aquatic balance contained within. If Britain had wildebeest and bison constantly charging from one end to the other we'd be living in a dustbowl as well.

Build areas that give the bison, elephant and rhino everything they want in one place. That way, they won't have to roam and destroy looking for food and water.

How about centipedes? If there's no justification for people in urban areas having five-litre off-road vehicles, there's no justification for a creature having one hundred legs in a fragile environment like the jungle. Every centipede must be rounded up, brought into the Red Cross vets and have every second leg removed (alternate sides obviously or they'll be walking round in circles.)

Creatures need to start living more in harmony with the planet, like alligators. Alligators get little birds to clean their teeth for them, in order to save on toothpaste packaging and the cost of recycling used toothbrushes. Apparently the first bird ever to perform this task got the alligator to put his tadger in the mouth of a lion by way of an insurance policy.

This is where my theories concerning the melting of the icecaps and saving Africa merge. Am I the only person who can see the ludicrous contradiction in half the world panicking about flooding and losing whole cities to the sea whilst people in Africa die because of drought induced famine? This, again, is where diverting the sea through Africa helps. New York stays above land and Africa gets all the water it needs for its crops. The constant flow of cold seawater through Africa will also help cool the planet down a bit.

Don't just re-direct the ice that's melting through Africa; force the issue. Deliberately melt every iceberg left on this planet and be done with it. Africa is really, really big and if we're not careful the new canals could end up using too much water and then Europe, America and Australia would find themselves dry as a bone. Famine would set in as the crops failed and the stock market crashed. Then all the new crops grown in Africa would have to be sent back to us as part of the aid effort. Comic Relief would have to move to Africa, where Lenny Henry will show videos of kids in Basingstoke having to walk to Andover to find water.

I've a theory that the ice age made the world so cold that it's simply taken all this time for it to get back to its normal temperature. The world was never meant to be as cold as it got, and it was only the invention of CFCs that rescued this planet from its deep freeze nightmare.

If sea levels are rising why don't we just raise the land? Lower the areas that are going to flood anyway and pile it all on top of the bits that aren't. In short, mountains. Mountains are cool. They look cool, water can't run up them and housing also benefits.

Take a plot of land that can accommodate a thousand houses. Build a mountain on it, and then build houses all up one side, and then down the other. My calculations show that you could build loads more houses on that plot. The houses could be built into the mountain like hobbits' houses, and buses and taxis could be replaced by environmentally friendly cable cars.

Make all burglars live at the top of the mountain. They're far less likely to break in and steal your tele if they've then got to carry it all the way up the mountain. When the

England football team has a game coming up at high altitude there will be lots of mountains for them to train on.

More mountains mean more snow. If we build them high enough we might even get some sort of ski resort going. With all the water running down off the mountains we could maybe build some white-water canoeing facilities or a crafty raft centre.

So, let's recap. We build new canals and rivers through Africa, populate them with fish, breed crocodiles specifically for meat, and open up McDonald's restaurants on the riverbank. The McCroc burger, with a free side of western pensioner McNuggets, fries, coke and a gun for the kids in case anti-government rebels turn up.

If working-class votes do more damage than good, do we let just upper and middle-class people vote? No. Middle-class people are even worse. They lack the edge, drive and hardness of the working-classes and the class or arrogance of the upper-classes. They spend their life working every hour God sends so they can drink fine wines, live in big houses, drive nice cars and send their kids to private schools, whilst claiming they're all Socialists because they read The Guardian and oppose the war. The answer is demotion, promotion, or death.

There are three kinds of middle-class people; clever, stupid, and annoying. Promote the clever wealthy people to the upper classes, and demote the divvy ones back into the working classes. All the annoying ones, i.e. the ones with "causes" must die.

Yes, I know. It's funny how many of my enlightened theories tend to end up with mass murder or compulsory suicide. "Ian!" I hear you scream, "There's so much we can learn from you, but do so many people have to die?"

You're right. Sometimes, disabling or mutilation will suffice. Besides, it's not as if I want to kill everybody. In a world run by me many, many people will be allowed to live, and, free from all the crap they had to deal with before, will go on to enjoy blissfully happy, serene, stress free, graceful lives, like a swan who's just had some fishing tackle removed from its throat.

I'd only kill the ones who deserve it, and nobody deserves it more than middle-class people with causes. I call them "pseudo really intelligent cause-orientated know-it-alls" or "PRICKs" for short.

Everywhere you go there's a PRICK waiting behind a bush to jump out and lecture you for something you're doing wrong. Not content with screwing up their own lives and traumatising their own children they relentlessly ram their stupid theories down your throat as well.

If you feed your kid one gram of salt they'll get high blood pressure, give them a chocolate bar and they'll get diabetes, let them out in the sun and they'll get cancer. Give them a cheeseburger and they're going to have a heart attack and if you let your kid stray further than a hundred yards from the house you might as well paint a big target on its arse for the local paedophile.

And boy, do PRICKs love the environment. Many of them can't remember what they did with their lives before global warming came along. The kettle has to be filled with just the right amount of water for one cup. A light left on for one hour is tantamount to the murder of an Amazonian rain-child and anyone who flies on a plane is an eco-war criminal who should be tried before The Hague.

A PRICK wakes up one morning and decides to stick up for an entire group of people who hate them even more than me. They'll walk around telling people to take England flags down because "Muslims find it offensive," when most of them don't.

A PRICK will tell you that "baa-baa black sheep" is a racist nursery rhyme, that "policeman" is sexist, and that nativity plays should be banned. A PRICK will tell you all roads should have a twenty miles an hour speed limit, but if you made them 20mph they'd launch a new campaign to make them 15mph.

A PRICK waits around town centre construction projects demanding to know what's going on, and complaining to the council if he sees somebody using a disc-cutter without a mask. A PRICK refers to shops run by Asians as "ethnic minority stores," oblivious to the fact they're just finding a PC way to say "Paki shop."

A PRICK says things like, "I have such a problem with authority," like it makes them some kind of fashionably flawed maverick. In truth, everybody has a problem with authority. Nobody likes being told what to do, but accepting it as part and parcel of life is all part of graduating from child to adult. So grow up, PRICK.

A PRICK has a nervous breakdown every time he sees somebody smoking a cigarette, and campaigns relentlessly for higher taxes on alcohol to fight binge drinking.

If you triple the taxation on alcohol, three things will happen:

One. Every single pub, social club, and nightclub in Britain will be robbed on a weekly basis.

Two. Smuggling of cheap booze from France will

increase tenfold overnight, meaning a huge rise in the cost of policing our borders and hundreds of millions a year sucked out of our economy and into France.

Three. Every single council estate in Britain will have at least one home-brew man or woman. These people, in addition to claiming their dole money, housing benefit and child support will spend their day brewing unrefined 12% gut rot home brew and 50% moonshine and selling it to all the drinkers on the estate.

The kids will spend most of their evening delivering home brew around the estate instead of hanging around on corners hassling people, but having done that they'll spend the money they've earned on drugs and gut rot and then smash the estate up.

The end result will be the problem-drinkers getting twice as drunk, twice as quick, causing twice as much trouble, having twice as many fights, with twice the damage to their health. Not only that, with gut rot going for less than a pound a litre they'll have twice as much money to spend on drugs. Fantastic. Today's edition of Sesame Street – The Politics Edition was brought to you by the letters P,R,I,C, and K, and by the number 69 (snigger, chortle.)

Come on. Let's kill the PRICKs, you know you want to. Years ago, in the days when people were locked in the tower, they would kill people by ramming a red-hot poker up their bum. Ouch. Imagine the smell. Having given the matter my full consideration, this is the only punishment I feel is appropriate.

What are we going to do with all these bodies? Simple. We cremate them, and use the ashes as ballast, mixing it with the snot from the Snot-hoover™ clinics to make eco-compost, which will be shipped to Africa to help grow grain and potatoes in beer-famine-hit areas.

So who should be allowed to vote? Again, it's quite simple. Anybody who passes the knowledge test and earns more than £100,000 per year should be allowed to vote. How easy was that? Simplicity, simplicity, simplicity.

And there you have it. Just like that. The answers to all of life's problems. Didn't take long did it?

Earlier I spoke of being mugged by a brown polar bear. You want to know why polar bears are white? It's because they're bloody freezing. When polar bears attack humans, it's not because they're after food or protecting their young. What they're after is a lift. "What are you running away for? Take me with you! Look at me! I'm so cold I look like a snowball!" This is why I was mugged by a brown polar bear; you bring one to England and it returns to its normal colour.

Life is not always just about the big problems. Sometimes it's the small problems that can be more damaging. Silly problems can ruin your life, but they're not as bad as embarrassing problems, such as Schwarzblink-Johnnson Syndrome (SJD), otherwise known as Taxi Driver Scrotum.

SJD sufferers have scrotums which overheat and stretch. Long car journeys and working in stuffy offices can trigger an attack. If your scrotum reaches the right temperature it can stretch to twelve times its normal size. I saw a bloke pull his scrotum over his head once. One poor man with similar problems was skinny-dipping off Torquay when he was mistaken for a jellyfish and tasered by the local sub-aqua club.

Sufferers are unable to wear shorts during summer and

are routinely pulled over at customs to see if they have drugs secluded in the folds of their scrotilia.

When sufferers have an attack, they follow something called the "Al Dente Procedure." When pasta is cooked you can tell if it's al dente i.e. ready, by throwing it at a wall. If it sticks, it's cooked.

If you think you might be overheating, stand parallel to your bedroom wall, drop your pants and swing your scrotum against the wall. If it sticks you are in trouble, and rapid action needed. DO NOT put ice on it as this can give you varicose veins in your willy; great for pleasuring your partner, but erections can become excruciatingly painful. The only treatment available for varicose willy involves ripping the vein out like cable from a wall.

Firstly, Sellotape your willy to your belly. Point a fan at your scrotum and turn it on, stopping every two minutes to dip your sack into a basin of room temperature water. That night, sleep with a peeled potato in your pants to absorb any excess salt in your scrotum, then consult a registered physio for remedial work.

Throughout my recommendations in this book there is one policy that, above all, needs to be implemented. The amount of people I have advocated killing simply wouldn't be possible without capital punishment. We need to start hanging people again, in public, or beheading them.

When it's my turn to be executed (I'm bound to do something stupid enough sooner or later) I wish to be beheaded, (Jonny Wilkinson is to kick my head off Tower Bridge, remember) like so many kings and queens before me. I'll regale the audience with witty anecdotes, ask the executioner for a good clean cut, and kneel before the block as my pals launch a daring rescue mission in vain.

Think of the drama and sense of occasion as my head plops into the basket, my head continuing to talk for at least two minutes whilst my body gets up and runs around like a chicken. My pumpkin shaped bonce will then be handed to a local necrophiliac chapter, where they can spend a couple of days trying to fuck-start my head before handing it back to be placed on a spike outside the Tower of London. There it will glare intently at the London public till my eyes fall out and my ears fold over like flowers wilting in the autumn sunshine. Then Jonny can kick it.

During the olden days thousands would congregate to watch people being beheaded or hanged. It was a chance for people to mix, let their hair down and enjoy the show. This is precisely the kind of event that could help restore the community spirit that larger cities like London now lack. The reason our prisons are overcrowded is that we don't kill enough people.

You want to eliminate prison over-crowding? Here's what you do. If a prison has a capacity of 20,000, you reach that capacity, and a local drug dealer gets caught with a boot full of drugs, don't let him go, just execute the baddest prisoner in the prison to make room for your new inmate.

When any prison is full, the baddest motherfucker will then put the word out on the street that nobody is to get caught committing any crime or he'll have their entire family killed before he goes to the gallows.

If we can offer suicidal or terminally ill people financial incentives to pop their clogs, why not offer it to inmates if they volunteer for execution? Their family will get some cash with which to break out of the cycle they're in and we'll save a fortune in prison costs. Surely exploring the after-life is more attractive than sitting in a cell for fifty years?

Many people wouldn't have the death penalty in this country because an innocent person might get killed, but innocent people get killed every day; it doesn't make something a bad idea.

Yes, yes, yes, all right, in America they have the death penalty and one of the highest murder rates in the world. This is because only a tiny percentage of people sent to death row are actually killed. Most spend their whole life on death row, filing appeal after appeal. Again, offer the villain twenty thousand for his family if he stops fannying about and takes his punishment; it's a fraction of the money the lawyers make.

I don't have a sweeping conclusion to come to. This entire book has been chapter one and conclusion all rolled into one. If we put aside ego, prejudice, ultra-sensitivity and outdated political dogma, I'm convinced the answers are out there. In Korea, the police have found blind people have an extraordinary sense of smell, and use them at airports to sniff for drugs. In Britain, people would see it as disrespectful to ask the blind to do this. There would be outrage. In Korea, however, this is seen as a vital and important role for blind people; they have, after all, eaten all the dogs.

"Always leaving them laughing," is as good a way as any to finish. So I'm going to leave you with a joke; the best I've got.

A man, let's call him John, walks down the street feeling sorry for himself. He's out of work and his wife has long since left him and taken the kids. With little money left in the bank, he's taking a walk to clear his head.

"Hello, John!" He looks up to see an old workmate. They used to be quite good friends.

"All right, Dave," he mumbles.

"What's wrong with you?"

"Everything. Out of work, missus has fucked off, I've a hundred pound left, and that's about it."

"Oh dear," says Dave. Now Dave is one of those annoyingly happy people that never seems to be down and always sees the positive in everything. "You know what you need? A good night out and a good win at the bookies. This could be your lucky day. What are you doing tonight?"

"Nothing."

"Get your hundred pounds," says Dave, "and meet me here later. No questions. Just meet me here at eight."

John is not convinced, but as he watches his mate walking away he decides that he's got little to lose, and maybe his luck is due for a change. That night he turns up at eight to meet his mate. Dave arrives.

"Okay. Put me out of my misery. Where are we going?"

"Bear-shagging."

"What?"

"It's obviously illegal, don't tell anybody for fuck's sake, but they have bear shagging contests, on which you can bet. There's a bar there and bookmakers and everything, and I've got a tip. Red Bear Number 5. I've been told this thing shags for fun. It can't get beat. You stick your hundred on that, you're quids-in."

After much persuading, John finally agrees to go along. He gets a beer, gives his hundred pounds to Dave, who goes to the bookies, and gets odds of ten to one. The bears come out.

"There he is!" whispers Dave loudly.

Red Bear Number 5 comes out and he is indeed a stunning looking specimen. Huge and physically imposing, he looks supremely confident. The female bears line up. The male bears line up behind them.

The gun goes and the male bears mount up and begin to shag their partner. All except Red Bear Number 5. As the others all get on with the job in hand, Red Bear Number 5 wanders lazily over to the corner, sits down and starts to watch.

John is concerned. "What the fuck is he doing?" Dave is also concerned. "I don't know."

With that, Red Bear Number 5 begins to masturbate furiously. Clearly enjoying the huge bear-bonk unfolding in front of him, he sets about himself with gusto. John is now extremely concerned. "Please tell me that bear is not wanking itself off."

Dave is speechless. The other bears are now well into their stride and shagging like demons. "Do something!" yells John.

The crowd are now watching Red Bear Number 5 with glee. Howls of laughter ring round the arena. Red Bear Number 5 pauses. His eyes cross as he comes like a cannon, spraying all the other bears with grizzly growbag. The gun sounds, the other bears jump off their partners and exit the ring.

"I don't believe it," mutters John as he sits down and buries his head in his hands.

"Let me speak to someone," says Dave. "I'll check it out. Maybe we can get our money back." He wanders off through the crowd.

John is distraught. He looks in his pocket. A fiver and two pound coins. He doesn't get his dole till next week. What a mug!

Dave is running back through the crowd. "It's okay!" he yells. "It's okay!"

John jumps to his feet. "What? What's okay?"

"Red Bear Number 5!" says Dave. "He had a bye into the next round."